Micro Habits, Macro Results

Build Tiny Habits to Achieve Daily Success and Lasting Change

Adam C Norton

Copyright © 2024 by Adam C Norton

All rights reserved.

No portion of this book may be reproduced in any form without written permission from the publisher or author, except as permitted by U.S. copyright law. This copyright page includes the necessary copyright notice, permissions request information, acknowledgements for the cover design, interior design, and editing, as well as the details of the first edition.

This publication is designed to provide accurate and authoritative information in regard to the subject matter covered. It is sold with the understanding that neither the author nor the publisher is engaged in rendering legal, investment, accounting or other professional services. While the publisher and author have used their best efforts in preparing this book, they make no representations or warranties with respect to the accuracy or completeness of the contents of this book and specifically disclaim any implied warranties of merchantability or fitness for a particular purpose. No warranty may be created or extended by sales representatives or written sales materials. The advice and strategies contained herein may not be suitable for your situation. You should consult with a professional when appropriate. Neither the publisher nor the author shall be liable for any loss of profit or any other commercial damages, including but not limited to special, incidental, consequential, personal, or other damages.

First Edition 2024

Introduction

Close your eyes for a moment and imagine the version of yourself you've always wanted to be. Maybe you're healthier, with energy that lasts all day. Maybe you're tackling that dream project you've put off for years. Maybe you're thriving in your relationships, confident, and in control of your life.

Now, imagine what it would feel like to know that the distance between you and that life isn't an unscalable mountain. It's not endless willpower or superhuman discipline.

It's something far simpler: a journey of small, intentional steps—steps that fit seamlessly into the life you're already living.

This book is your map for that journey. It's not about quick fixes or overwhelming overhauls. It's about discovering the profound power of micro habits—the tiny, repeatable actions that may seem inconsequential at first, but over time, create momentum so strong, it transforms everything. These habits don't demand perfection or extreme effort—they ask only for consistency, for one small step, and then another. But this isn't just about habits. It's about transformation.

Along the way, you'll uncover:

- The science behind why small changes have such a massive impact and how to work with your brain to build habits that stick.

- How a single micro habit can set off a ripple effect, improving not just one part of your life but many.

- Real-life stories of people who've gone from stuck to unstoppable, proving that even the smallest shifts can unlock extraordinary results.

- How to adapt your habits when life gets messy—because success doesn't come from avoiding challenges but from navigating them with resilience.

- Insights from around the globe, showing how habits shape cultures, communities, and lives in ways you've never imagined.

You won't just learn how to build better habits. You'll learn how to see change as an adventure, one that's uniquely yours—tailored to your goals, your challenges, your life. And as you move through this book, you'll start to feel it: the excitement of progress, the quiet satisfaction of showing up every day, and the growing belief that this time, you're truly on your way.

Every big transformation begins with a single decision: to take the first step. This is yours.

Are you ready to rewrite your story? Let's begin.

Contents

1. The Power of Micro Habits — 1
2. Micro Habits for Unconventional Goals — 9
3. The Science Behind Small Changes — 15
4. The Role of Play and Experimentation in Habit-Building — 19
5. The Habit Loop — 25
6. Setting the Stage for Success — 29
7. The Science of Motivation — 35
8. The 1% Rule — 41
9. Habits and Decision Fatigue — 49
10. The Ripple Effect — 57
11. Seasonal Habits and the Rhythms of Life — 65
12. Habit Stacking — 73
13. Tracking Progress and Staying Motivated — 81
14. Overcoming Obstacles — 89
15. The Art of Starting Over — 95
16. Building Resilience — 101
17. Habits in Extreme Situations — 107

18.	Habit Alignment for Team and Families	115
19.	Cultural and Global Perspectives on Habits	119
20.	The Role of Accountability	125
21.	Mindset Matters	133
22.	The Habits of Highly Adaptable People	141
23.	The Long Game	149
24.	Mastering Habit Synergy	155

The Power of Micro Habits

When I first encountered the idea of micro habits, I didn't quite get it. The concept sounded abstract—like something you'd read about in a psychology journal or hear from a motivational speaker. But the deeper I delved, the more it clicked: these tiny actions have extraordinary power. They're not just small—they're mighty.

The science is clear. Our brains are wired to favor simplicity and efficiency. When you embed small, repeatable actions into your daily life, you're not just making incremental changes—you're reshaping your neural pathways. Over time, these seemingly minor tweaks create a ripple effect that transforms how you think, act, and succeed.

Micro habits are the foundation of transformation: tiny, consistent actions that, when repeated, lead to lasting change. At first glance, they may seem insignificant—like drinking a single glass of water upon waking or writing one sentence a day. However, their simplicity is their strength. By requiring minimal effort, these actions bypass the brain's resistance to change, allowing consistency to take hold. Over time, micro habits accumulate, creating momentum that leads to meaningful and lasting transformation. For a deeper dive into the science that makes these habits so effective, see the remainder of this chapter.

Why Small Changes Work

Why do micro habits work so well? It boils down to behavioral psychology. They leverage two fundamental principles: **minimal resistance and momentum.**

First, when a task feels easy, you're less likely to resist it. Compare "write a book" to "write one sentence." Which one feels achievable right now? By starting small, you eliminate the mental friction that often comes with big, intimidating goals.

Second, small actions create momentum. Once you start, it's easier to keep going. Psychologists call this the "endowed progress effect." It's the reason loyalty cards with a few stamps already marked make you more likely to complete them. The progress, no matter how small, keeps you engaged.

Real-World Stories of Micro Habits in Action

Meet Layla, a project manager who felt like she was treading water in her career. Every day, she went through the motions—meetings, emails, endless spreadsheets—yet the spark she once had for her work had faded. For years, she'd dreamed of transitioning into tech, drawn to the creativity and innovation of coding. But every time she thought about taking that leap, doubts crept in: *What if I'm not smart enough? Where would I even begin?* The fear of failure paralyzed her before she could even start.

One evening, after yet another frustrating day at work, Layla stumbled upon an article about micro habits. The idea intrigued her—small, consistent actions leading to big results? It seemed almost too simple. But as she sat there, scrolling through job listings for roles she didn't feel qualified for, something clicked. What if she could dip her toes in, just to see if coding was even for her? No pressure, no grand plan—just five minutes a day to try.

The next evening, she opened a free coding tutorial online. The task was basic: write a line of code to display "Hello, World!" on the screen. It took her five minutes. She stared at the words on her screen and laughed at how small an accomplishment it was—but for the first time in a while, she felt a glimmer of excitement.

At first, the five-minute practice was almost comical in its simplicity. Some evenings, she'd close her laptop right after completing a single exercise. But then something unexpected happened: five minutes didn't feel like enough. By the second week, she found herself staying longer, eager to solve the next problem or tweak her code. Five minutes stretched into ten, then fifteen, until coding became part of her evening rhythm.

Layla's confidence grew with each tiny milestone. She completed small projects, like a calculator app and a to-do list. These weren't groundbreaking, but they were *hers*. Slowly, the self-doubt that had kept her stuck began to fade, replaced by curiosity and a growing sense of capability.

Six months later, Layla had built her first fully functional app: a budget tracker she could actually use in her daily life. It wasn't perfect, but it worked, and it symbolized how far she'd come from those first tentative five minutes. Encouraged, she started sharing her projects online and connecting with others in the tech community. Their feedback and support fueled her momentum, and she began to see a path forward.

A year after her journey began, Layla applied for a junior developer position at a local tech startup. She was terrified, but she also knew something she hadn't a year earlier: she had proof—both in her portfolio and in herself—that she could do this. The interview wasn't easy, but when the call came offering her the job, Layla realized something remarkable. It wasn't just her career that had changed—it was her entire mindset. She'd learned to trust herself, to embrace the small steps that led to big transformations.

Today, Layla still practices micro habits. She spends a few minutes each day learning a new coding language or refining her skills. But beyond the habits themselves, she's discovered something even more powerful: the belief that big dreams aren't impossible—they're just built one tiny, deliberate step at a time.

Consider Marcus, a father of three with a schedule that felt like a juggling act. Between long hours at work, shuttling kids to soccer games, and volunteering in his community, he barely had a moment to himself. By the time his head hit the pillow at night, he was too exhausted to think about exercise, let alone carve out time for it.

It wasn't always like this. In his younger years, Marcus had been active—hiking on weekends, shooting hoops with friends, and hitting the gym regularly. But as life got busier, his priorities shifted. He told himself he'd get back to it someday, when things calmed down. But "someday" never came, and the creeping fatigue and stiffness in his body were constant reminders of how far he'd drifted from the healthy, energetic man he once was.

One morning, after another restless night and a groggy start, Marcus caught sight of himself in the mirror. He barely recognized the reflection staring back at him—not just physically, but emotionally. He missed feeling strong, capable, and alive. He didn't have time for long workouts or gym memberships, but something had to change.

That day, a thought struck him: *What if I just started with one push-up?* It sounded ridiculous, almost too small to matter, but it felt manageable. Before hopping in the shower, he dropped to the floor and pushed out a single, shaky push-up. He laughed at how out of shape he felt—but it was a start.

The next day, he did it again. And the day after that. It wasn't about results at first; it was about proving to himself that he could show up, even for something so small. After a week, one push-up became two. Then three. The incremental progress felt almost trivial, but it gave Marcus a sense of control over his health he hadn't felt in years.

Weeks turned into months, and as Marcus's push-up count grew, so did his confidence. His kids noticed, too. "Can we try, Dad?" his youngest asked one morning, joining him on the floor. Soon, push-ups became a family affair, with his kids cheering each other on. The habit that had started as a single action turned into a bonding moment they all looked forward to.

By the end of the year, Marcus's fitness routine had grown well beyond push-ups. He added planks, jumping jacks, and other simple exercises that required no equipment and fit easily into his day. He didn't need an hour-long workout or a fancy gym membership—just a few dedicated minutes each morning.

But the changes weren't just physical. Marcus felt more energized, less stressed, and more present with his family. He had more patience at work and more stamina for playing with his kids in the backyard. His transformation wasn't just about building strength; it was about reclaiming a part of himself he thought he'd lost.

Today, Marcus still starts every morning with a quick workout. What began as a single push-up became a daily ritual—a reminder that no matter how busy life gets, there's always room to take care of yourself. And the best part? He's passed that lesson on to his kids, who now challenge *him* to keep up.

Why Micro Habits Outperform Big Goals

Traditional goal-setting often prioritizes outcomes over processes. You set an ambitious target—lose 20 pounds, write a novel, save $10,000—and fixate on reaching it. The problem? Goals like these can feel overwhelming, especially when progress is slow.

Micro habits flip the script. Instead of aiming for the summit, you focus on taking the first step.

These small actions:

- Build your confidence as you see tangible progress.

- Reduce decision fatigue by embedding habits into your routine.

- Lay the foundation for larger, sustained changes.

Here's another way to think about it: imagine you're piloting a plane. A minor course correction—just one degree—might seem trivial in the moment. But over thousands of miles, that small shift alters your entire trajectory, landing you somewhere entirely different.

How to Start Building Micro Habits

Ready to get started?

Here's a simple framework to help you build micro habits that stick:

1. **Start Small**: Choose an action so easy it's impossible to fail. Want to drink more water? Begin with one glass in the morning.

2. **Anchor to an Existing Routine**: Tie your habit to something you already do daily. For example, while brewing your morning coffee, drink that glass of water.

3. **Track Your Progress**: Keep a habit journal or use an app to record your success. Seeing those streaks grow can be incredibly motivating.

4. **Celebrate Wins**: Reinforce your habit with small rewards. Have you finished your daily push-ups? Treat yourself to a cup of your favorite tea.

As we move forward, remember this: micro habits thrive because they fit seamlessly into the life you already have. They don't demand perfection or extraordinary effort. They ask only for one small step, repeated consistently.

So, what's the first micro habit you'll commit to? Maybe it's a push-up, a glass of water, or a single sentence. Whatever it is, start now. Small steps lead to big transformations.

Micro Habits for Unconventional Goals

When most people think about habits, they envision straightforward goals: getting fit, waking up earlier, or eating healthier. These are the poster children of the habit-building world, and for good reason. They're relatable, tangible, and easy to measure. But habits are far more versatile than that. What if, instead, you could use micro habits to improve something less obvious—like nurturing your creativity, becoming a better conversationalist, or fostering a deeper connection with nature? These unconventional goals, often overlooked, can be just as life-changing, if not more so, because they tap into the unique corners of who you are and what makes life meaningful.

Let's take a step beyond the typical and explore how micro habits can help us achieve goals that are off the beaten path. By embracing creativity, curiosity, and intention, you can unlock areas of growth you never thought possible.

The Hidden Power of Unconventional Goals

When Lorain was a child, her curiosity for the stars was insatiable. She'd spend hours reading about planets and constellations, her imagination soaring as she pictured herself as an astronaut. But as she grew older, life happened. College, a career in finance, and the busy routines of adulthood swept her dreams to the side. By her early thirties, she realized she hadn't looked through a telescope since she was a teenager.

One evening, while scrolling through her phone, Lorain stumbled across an article about habit-building. The idea of micro habits—small, consistent actions—intrigued her. Could she rekindle her love of astronomy with something so simple? She decided to find out.

As discussed in Chapter 2, starting small is the cornerstone of sustainable habits. For Lorain, stepping outside each night for just a few minutes rekindled her passion for stargazing. At first, she felt silly. She didn't know the names of constellations anymore, and city lights often dimmed the stars. But as she kept showing up, something changed. She downloaded a stargazing app and started identifying constellations. On weekends, she drove out to darker areas for better views. Within months, her five-minute nightly habit had reignited her passion. She joined a local astronomy club and even saved up for a telescope. Lorain wasn't just looking at stars; she was reconnecting with a piece of herself.

The lesson? Unconventional goals are worth pursuing because they bring us closer to what makes life rich and fulfilling. Habits aren't just about productivity or health—they're about becoming the person you want to be.

Habits to Nurture Creativity

Creativity often feels elusive, a flash of inspiration rather than something you can cultivate. But in reality, creativity thrives on consistency. Small, intentional habits can help you nurture this invaluable skill.

Take Monroe, a software engineer who always envied his artist friends. He'd tell himself he wasn't creative, but deep down, he wanted to learn how to draw. Instead of waiting for inspiration, Monroe started with a micro habit: drawing one doodle a day. It didn't matter if it was a stick figure or a squiggle—what mattered was that he picked up the pen.

Monroe's initial doodles were far from perfect, but he found joy in the process. Over time, his confidence grew, and he began experimenting with shading and perspective, transforming his simple habit into a profound source of creative expression. By the end of the year, Monroe's walls were adorned with his artwork, from abstract sketches to detailed landscapes. He even gave a few pieces as gifts to friends and family, who were amazed at his progress. Through this small, consistent habit, Monroe not only unlocked a hidden talent but also found a new passion that enriched his life in ways he never anticipated.

Building Connection Through Micro Habits

Sometimes the most unconventional goals are the ones that strengthen our relationships. Being a better listener, expressing gratitude, or even remembering someone's favorite coffee order can deepen connections in profound ways.

Consider Randy, a busy entrepreneur who often found himself distracted during conversations. He wanted to improve his relationships, but his packed schedule left little room for grand gestures. Instead, Randy started a micro habit: at the end of each day, he'd write down one meaningful thing he'd learned about someone that day.

At first, it was small details: "Sarah's favorite movie is Jurassic Park," or "Jeff's daughter just started kindergarten." But as the habit continued, Randy noticed a shift. When he saw Sarah next, he asked her why she loved that movie. Her face lit up as they shared a conversation beyond work. With Jeff, he followed up about his daughter's school experience, earning an appreciative smile.

What began as a simple act of noting details turned into deeper, more meaningful interactions. Randy's relationships flourished, not because he had more time, but because he paid attention.

Environmental Stewardship Through Small Actions

Unconventional goals often extend beyond ourselves. What about habits that make the world a better place? Small, eco-friendly actions can ripple out into significant change.

Maya felt overwhelmed by the scale of climate change, but she started with one small habit: carrying a reusable water bottle. This modest change snowballed into broader actions that inspired those around her, showcasing how small, eco-friendly choices can create a ripple effect. She began bringing reusable bags to the store and saying no to single-use plastics. Over time, Maya's choices inspired her friends and coworkers to follow suit. By focusing on one small habit, Maya became a role model for sustainable living.

The Ripple Effect of Unconventional Habits

The beauty of these goals lies in their unexpected rewards. They don't just enrich your life—they change how you see the world. Lorain's stargazing didn't just reconnect her with astronomy; it reminded her of the vastness of the universe and her place in it. Monroe's drawings became a source of joy and connection as he gifted them to friends. Randy's listening habit transformed his relationships, making him a more empathetic leader.

Unconventional goals remind us that the best habits often transcend measurable outcomes. They reconnect us with our passions, strengthen our relationships, and deepen our connection to the world around us. By embracing the unconventional, you create a life that's not just productive but profoundly meaningful.

The Science Behind Small Changes

When you imagine forming a habit, it might seem as simple as repeating an action until it feels natural. But beneath every habit lies a fascinating transformation within your brain—a process as complex as it is powerful. Understanding the science behind this transformation can not only deepen your appreciation for habits but also give you the tools to shape them with precision.

At the center of this process is your brain's remarkable ability to adapt through **neuroplasticity**. Think of neuroplasticity as the brain's version of remodeling. Every action you repeat strengthens the connections between neurons responsible for that behavior, much like a trail becomes more defined as hikers tread it again and again. When you brush your teeth without thinking or automatically reach for your phone when it buzzes, you're seeing the effects of these well-worn neural pathways.

The Brain's Habit Machinery

Habits don't just happen; they're managed by specific areas of the brain. The **basal ganglia**, for example, acts as the brain's automation hub. It's responsible for taking repeated actions—like tying your shoes or driving a familiar route—and turning them into routines that run on autopilot. This frees up your prefrontal cortex, the part of your brain responsible for decision-making and willpower, to focus on more pressing matters.

Imagine you're learning to ride a bike. At first, your prefrontal cortex works overtime, processing every wobble, every brake, every adjustment to the handlebars. But as you practice, the basal ganglia takes over. The motions become fluid and natural, requiring almost no conscious thought. Over time, this shift in control is what makes habits feel effortless.

The handoff between these parts of the brain explains why starting a new habit often feels mentally taxing. It's not because you're bad at it—it's because your brain hasn't yet built the shortcuts that make it automatic. This insight is crucial: the struggle isn't a sign of failure; it's evidence that your brain is learning.

Dopamine: The Brain's Habit Reinforcer

If the basal ganglia is the brain's automation center, **dopamine** is its motivator. Often called the "feel-good chemical," dopamine surges in your brain whenever you encounter something rewarding. But what's particularly interesting about dopamine is its role in creating cravings.

Imagine you've established a habit of going for a morning run. At first, you likely motivated yourself with the promise of a long-term reward—improved fitness, more energy, better health. But as the habit took hold, you started noticing a shift. Even before you step outside, just lacing up your running shoes sparks a sense of anticipation. That's dopamine at work, linking the act of putting on your shoes to the endorphin rush you feel after a run. Over time, this anticipation becomes so strong that the shoes themselves act as a cue, triggering your routine.

This process is why habits can feel so compelling—and why bad habits can be so hard to break. Whether it's the ping of a text message or the smell of fresh pastries, dopamine ensures that your brain remembers the reward and craves it again and again. But here's the good news: you can use this same process to your advantage.

Rewiring Your Brain

One of the most exciting discoveries in neuroscience is that your brain is always changing. This **neuroplasticity** is what makes breaking old habits and forming new ones possible. But it also explains why the process can feel slow. Breaking an old habit doesn't erase its neural pathway—it simply weakens it. Imagine a grass-covered trail. If you stop walking it, the grass will grow back over time, making the path harder to see. Meanwhile, creating a new habit is like carving out a fresh trail, requiring consistent effort until it becomes well-defined.

This dual process—weakening old pathways and strengthening new ones—is why replacing a bad habit with a good one is often more effective than trying to "quit" cold turkey. For example, if you're trying to stop snacking late at night, replacing chips with a healthier option like fruit allows your brain to maintain the cue and routine while gradually rewiring the reward.

How to Work With Your Brain

To make the most of your brain's natural tendencies, focus on consistency over intensity. Think of every repetition as a vote for the habit you want to establish. Even tiny actions—like writing one sentence, meditating for a minute, or doing a single push-up—signal to your brain that this behavior matters.

Instead of battling your brain, collaborate with it. Create environments that make positive cues obvious and bad cues invisible. Celebrate small wins to flood your brain with dopamine, reinforcing your efforts. And when the process feels slow, remind yourself: each repetition is a step closer to a brain wired for success.

The Science of Transformation

The science behind small changes lays the groundwork for understanding how our actions shape our lives. To truly leverage this knowledge, we need to explore the framework that governs all habits. This is where the Habit Loop comes in—a process that reveals how habits form, why they persist, and how we can reshape them to serve our goals.

The Role of Play and Experimentation in Habit-Building

When you think about building habits, the words that might come to mind are "discipline," "commitment," and "focus." These are undeniably important, but they often make the process feel rigid and joyless. What if habit-building could feel less like a chore and more like a game? What if, instead of worrying about failure, you approached your habits with a sense of play and curiosity? This mindset can transform the way you think about personal growth, making the process not only more effective but also more enjoyable.

Play and experimentation add an element of creativity and flexibility to the discipline of habit formation, offering a stark contrast to the rigidity of traditional approaches. While conventional habit-building often emphasizes strict schedules and unwavering adherence to routines, a playful mindset invites exploration and adaptability. It encourages a process of trial and error, where the focus shifts from avoiding mistakes to discovering what truly works for you. This reframing transforms habit-building into an engaging journey rather than a stringent task. They allow you to explore what works, adapt to changing circumstances, and remain motivated even when progress feels slow. By treating habit-building as a playful experiment rather than a test of willpower, you'll open up a world of possibilities.

The Freedom to Play

As a child, Lisa loved puzzles. She would spend hours piecing together complex jigsaws, relishing the satisfaction of seeing the bigger picture emerge. But as an adult, her life had become a puzzle of a different kind—balancing work, family, and personal goals often left her feeling drained. When she decided to focus on improving her health, the idea of starting another "serious" routine felt overwhelming.

That's when she remembered the joy of puzzles. What if she treated her health goals as a game instead of a burden? Lisa set out to "gamify" her habits, assigning herself points for every healthy action she took. Drinking a glass of water earned her one point. A morning walk scored five. Trying a new vegetable was worth ten. At the end of each week, she tallied her score and rewarded herself with something small but meaningful, like a new book or a guilt-free afternoon nap.

This playful approach reignited Lisa's motivation. Instead of feeling like a list of chores, her health goals became a series of fun challenges. She began looking forward to the little experiments she could try, like swapping her regular breakfast for a smoothie or seeing how far she could walk in ten minutes. The points weren't the real reward—it was the spark of joy and creativity that came with treating her habits as a game.

Experimenting Without Fear

Experimenting isn't just about finding what works; it's about building resilience through adaptability. When you allow yourself to play with different approaches, each trial—whether successful or not—teaches you something valuable about your process. This mindset transforms perceived failures into stepping stones for growth, reinforcing your ability to adapt in any situation.

One of the biggest obstacles in habit-building is the fear of failure. If you set a goal to meditate daily and miss a day, it can feel like you've failed entirely. But experimentation reframes failure as data. Each setback becomes an opportunity to learn what works for you and what doesn't.

Take Jonah, an overworked project manager who wanted to make reading a habit. He set an ambitious goal of finishing one book a week, but it quickly became overwhelming with his packed schedule. Frustrated, he decided to experiment instead. For one week, he committed to reading one page every night before bed. The next week, he tried listening to audiobooks during his commute. The following week, he spent his lunch break reading short stories instead of scrolling through his phone.

Through this process, Jonah discovered that reading before bed wasn't ideal—he often fell asleep before finishing a page. Audiobooks, however, turned his commutes into something he looked forward to, while lunchtime reading allowed him to relax and recharge. By experimenting with different methods, Jonah found an approach that fit seamlessly into his life, turning reading into a habit he genuinely enjoyed.

The Science of Play

Play isn't just for fun—it's a powerful tool for learning and adaptation. Neuroscience shows that play activates the brain's reward system, releasing dopamine and fostering creativity. When you approach habits playfully, you're more likely to stick with them because they feel rewarding in the moment.

Imagine experimenting with fitness by trying a new activity every week: yoga, dance, rock climbing, or even hula hooping. The variety keeps the habit fresh and exciting, while the playful mindset reduces the pressure to "get it right." This exploratory approach doesn't just help you find what you love—it also builds resilience. If one approach doesn't work, you're already primed to try something else.

How to Gamify and Experiment with Habits

If you're ready to inject play and experimentation into your habit-building, here are some ways to get started:

Create a Points System: Assign point values to different actions and track your score. Treat yourself to small rewards when you reach a certain threshold.

Try Mini Challenges: Commit to a short-term habit experiment, like drinking only water for three days or writing 100 words daily for a week. Reflect on how it felt and what you learned.

Change the Environment: Experiment with your surroundings. If you've been struggling to read more, create a cozy reading nook and see how it affects your behavior.

Role-Play: Imagine yourself as a character—a chef trying out new recipes, a fitness coach testing workouts, or a scientist analyzing data from your habit experiments.

A Playful Mindset in Action

Take Nadia, a recent college graduate who wanted to eat healthier. Her approach mirrored earlier ideas about gamification, using creativity and challenges to keep herself engaged. Instead of following a rigid meal plan, she turned her kitchen into a lab. She gave herself challenges like "make a vegetable dish with only five ingredients" or "create a new recipe using leftovers." Some experiments were flops (she learned the hard way that pickles and peanut butter don't mix), but others became staples in her diet. By approaching cooking as a game, Nadia not only improved her eating habits but also discovered a newfound passion for food.

Embracing Play for Lasting Change

Play and experimentation transform habit-building from a rigid process into a dynamic adventure. They encourage you to be curious, flexible, and forgiving of yourself. When you're not afraid to try new things, you open the door to unexpected discoveries—not just about what habits work, but about who you are and what brings you joy.

By embracing a playful mindset, you're not just building habits—you're creating a life filled with curiosity, creativity, and growth.

So go ahead: treat your habits as an experiment, and see where the game takes you.

The Habit Loop

At its core, every habit—good or bad—follows the same basic structure. This structure, known as the habit loop, consists of three components: the cue, the routine, and the reward. Understanding this loop is the key to unlocking how habits are formed, sustained, and, when necessary, changed.

Habits don't emerge randomly. They develop as the brain's way of conserving energy, automating repetitive tasks so we can focus on more complex decisions. By recognizing how the habit loop operates, you can take control of the habits that shape your life.

The Anatomy of a Habit

1. **Cue**: The trigger that initiates the habit. This could be anything—a specific time of day, an emotional state, or an environmental cue.

    - *Example*: Walking into your kitchen and seeing a coffee maker might trigger your habit of brewing coffee.

2. **Routine**: The behavior or action you perform in response to the cue. This is the habit itself.

    - *Example*: After seeing the coffee maker, you brew and

drink a cup of coffee.

3. **Reward**: The benefit or satisfaction you gain from completing the habit. Rewards reinforce the habit loop, making it more likely you'll repeat the behavior in the future.

    - *Example*: Drinking coffee provides the reward of feeling alert and energized.

This loop—cue, routine, reward—repeats itself until the behavior becomes automatic.

Real-Life Examples of the Habit Loop

A Morning Alarm:

- *Cue*: Your alarm clock rings at 6:00 a.m.

- *Routine*: You immediately reach for your phone and scroll through social media.

- *Reward*: You experience a brief distraction from the grogginess of waking up.

The Office Candy Bowl:

- *Cue*: Walking past a candy bowl at work.

- *Routine*: Grabbing a piece of candy and eating it.

- *Reward*: A small burst of pleasure from the sugar.

Exercise as a Habit:

- *Cue*: Putting on your workout clothes.
- *Routine*: Heading out for a 20-minute jog.
- *Reward*: The endorphins and sense of accomplishment you feel afterward.

By dissecting these examples, it's easy to see how habits are reinforced through repetition of the loop.

Why the Habit Loop Matters

The habit loop explains why some behaviors feel effortless while others feel like a constant struggle. Once a habit is established, the cue triggers the routine automatically—your brain doesn't need to think about it.

This can be both a blessing and a challenge. While helpful habits like brushing your teeth or exercising become automatic, unhelpful ones—like procrastination or overeating—can also embed themselves into your routine. The good news? The habit loop gives you a framework for reshaping your habits.

How to Change a Habit Using the Loop

To change a habit, you don't need to eliminate the entire loop—you just need to adjust one of its components.

1. **Identify the Cue**: Pay attention to what triggers the habit. Is it a specific time, place, or feeling?
    - *Example*: If snacking late at night is your habit, the cue

might be boredom or watching TV.

2. **Replace the Routine**: Instead of trying to suppress the habit, swap the routine for a healthier behavior.

    - *Example*: When the urge to snack strikes, try drinking a glass of water or doing a brief stretch.

3. **Reinforce the Reward**: Make sure the new behavior still provides a satisfying reward.

    - *Example*: If the snack was your way of relaxing, find a new reward, like a calming tea or a quick meditation.

Setting the Foundation for Habit Formation

By understanding the habit loop, you gain the ability to take control of your behavior. Start by observing the cues, routines, and rewards in your own life. Which loops serve you well? Which ones hold you back?

This chapter lays the groundwork for deeper strategies explored later in the book. Concepts like habit stacking and accountability build on this understanding, helping you turn awareness into action.

The habit loop isn't just a theory—it's a tool for creating the habits that will define your success. The next step is learning how to set yourself up for that success.

Setting the Stage for Success

Success doesn't happen by accident—it's the result of preparation and intentionality. When it comes to building lasting habits, your environment, mindset, and support systems play a crucial role. By setting the stage for success, you make it easier to stay consistent and overcome challenges.

Think of your habits as seeds. Even the healthiest seed won't thrive in poor soil. But when you plant it in rich, fertile ground, provide the right amount of sunlight, and tend to it consistently, it flourishes. Similarly, setting the right conditions for your habits can make the difference between thriving and fizzling out.

The Role of Environment in Habit Formation

Your environment has a powerful influence on your behavior. Whether you realize it or not, your surroundings are constantly sending cues that either encourage or discourage your habits. The key is to design your environment in a way that supports your goals.

Optimize for Success:

- **Make Good Habits Obvious**: Place cues for positive habits in plain sight. For example, leave a book on your bedside table to remind you to read before bed.

- **Reduce Friction**: Remove obstacles that make it harder to stick to your habits. If you want to exercise, lay out your workout clothes the night before.

- **Eliminate Temptations**: Minimize cues for bad habits. If you're trying to eat healthier, avoid keeping junk food within easy reach.

Ben, a graphic designer whose days were a whirlwind of deadlines, client meetings, and creative brainstorming sessions. His work was demanding but fulfilling, a blend of artistry and problem-solving that kept his mind constantly buzzing. Yet amidst the hustle of his daily grind, one thing always seemed to slip through the cracks: drinking water.

By mid-afternoon, Ben often felt sluggish and scattered, his creativity grinding to a halt. He'd blame the usual suspects—stress, lack of sleep, or too much coffee—but one day, while scrolling through yet another article about productivity hacks, he came across a surprising culprit: dehydration. The article claimed that even mild dehydration could sap energy and focus. Ben glanced at the empty coffee cup on his desk and realized he couldn't remember the last time he'd had plain water.

Determined to make a change, Ben tried setting lofty goals—eight glasses a day!—but by the second or third attempt, he'd fall back into his old patterns. He knew he needed a simpler approach, something he wouldn't forget during the chaos of his day. That's when he decided to try a micro habit.

The solution was almost laughably simple: each morning, as part of his routine, Ben placed a large water bottle on his desk. He didn't measure or set reminders—he just made the water visible and easy to reach. The first day, he drank half the bottle. The next day, a little more. Without even thinking about it, he began sipping as he worked.

What surprised Ben most was how quickly the habit took hold. The visible cue—a clear bottle filled with water—acted as a constant reminder, seamlessly weaving itself into his workday. Within weeks, drinking water became second nature, as automatic as checking his email or sketching a new design.

But the changes didn't stop there. As Ben stayed hydrated, he noticed subtle shifts in his energy and focus. The mid-afternoon fog lifted, and his creativity flowed more freely. His headaches—once a regular occurrence—became rare. Even his mood improved; he felt sharper, lighter, and more engaged in both his work and personal life.

Colleagues began to notice. "What's your secret?" one asked after seeing Ben power through a particularly intense project with ease. When he pointed to the water bottle, they laughed, but Ben knew it wasn't a joke. That small, unassuming bottle had become a symbol of his commitment to self-care in the midst of his busy life.

As weeks turned into months, Ben started tweaking other aspects of his routine. Inspired by how a simple habit had transformed his workday, he experimented with stretching during breaks and packing healthier lunches. Each new habit felt manageable, thanks to the confidence he'd gained from mastering the first one.

Today, Ben's water bottle still sits proudly on his desk—a quiet reminder of how small changes can lead to big results. What began as a tiny habit had rippled through his life, teaching him an invaluable lesson: even in the busiest moments, taking care of yourself isn't just possible—it's powerful.

Preparing Your Mindset

While your environment sets the stage, your mindset determines how you perform. A positive, flexible mindset helps you navigate setbacks and stay committed to your habits.

Focus on Progress, Not Perfection: Expecting perfection can lead to frustration and burnout. Instead, celebrate every step forward, no matter how small. Each day of progress reinforces your habits and builds momentum.

Reframe Challenges as Opportunities: When obstacles arise, view them as a chance to grow. For example, a missed workout might teach you to schedule exercise earlier in the day when your energy is higher.

Danielle, a busy parent of two energetic toddlers, often found herself craving a moment of calm in her chaotic mornings. She'd read about the benefits of meditation—how it could reduce stress, improve focus, and bring a sense of balance to the day—but finding time to practice in a household full of noise and demands felt impossible.

At first, she tried squeezing in five quiet minutes before her kids woke up. But more often than not, they'd wake earlier than expected, climbing into her lap just as she'd settled into her first deep breath. Frustrated, Danielle was tempted to abandon the idea altogether.

Then one morning, as her youngest giggled and mimicked her seated posture, she had a realization: *Why not make this something we do together?* Instead of seeing her children as a barrier to her meditation practice, she reframed them as part of it.

The next day, Danielle invited her kids to join her. She taught them simple breathing exercises—inhale deeply, exhale slowly—and encouraged them to sit cross-legged beside her. To her surprise, they loved it. At first, they could only manage a minute or two before getting restless, but that was enough to bring a moment of calm to their busy household.

Over time, the practice evolved into a cherished family ritual. They'd sit together each morning, focusing on their breaths or sharing what they were grateful for that day. Danielle still didn't get the quiet, solo meditation she'd originally envisioned, but what she gained was even better: a shared experience that brought her family closer.

What began as a personal goal turned into a meaningful tradition—a daily reminder that peace doesn't require perfection, only presence.

Shape Your Environment to Shape Your Behavior: Your surroundings send cues that encourage or discourage your habits.

By tweaking your environment, you can make the behaviors you want easier and more automatic.

Practical Adjustments:

- **Create Zones of Focus:** Dedicate specific spaces to specific habits. For example, designate one area of your home for exercise or meditation, making it a habit-friendly zone.

- **Leverage Convenience:** Place habit-related tools where they're easiest to access. For instance, keep a notepad and pen on your nightstand for journaling.

- **Control Your Digital Environment:** Reduce distractions by organizing your phone or computer. Turn off unnecessary notifications, and keep habit-building apps front and center.

A Foundation for Growth

Setting the stage for success isn't about perfection—it's about creating conditions that make it easier to thrive. By designing your environment, preparing your mindset, and building a support system, you create fertile ground for your habits to take root and grow.

This chapter serves as the launchpad for everything that follows. Armed with the right foundation, you'll be ready to dive into the specific strategies and techniques that will transform your habits—and your life.

The Science of Motivation

Motivation is often seen as the spark that ignites change. It's what gets you out of bed early for a workout, opens your notebook to brainstorm a new idea, or drives you to stick with a habit long enough for it to take root. But what happens when that spark fades?

Contrary to popular belief, motivation isn't something you either have or don't have. It's a dynamic force that ebbs and flows, influenced by both internal and external factors. Understanding how motivation works—and learning to harness it—can make all the difference in sustaining your habits.

The Two Types of Motivation

Motivation comes in two primary forms: **intrinsic** and **extrinsic**. Each plays a vital role in habit-building, but they work in different ways and serve different purposes.

Intrinsic Motivation: The Drive Within

Intrinsic motivation comes from within. It's the internal desire to do something because you find it personally rewarding or meaningful. When you're intrinsically motivated, you engage in an activity not for a reward or external validation, but because it aligns with your values, sparks joy or satisfies your curiosity.

Imagine Isabella, a language enthusiast learning Spanish. She doesn't need external rewards to motivate her—she simply loves the process of discovering new words, practicing pronunciation, and connecting with a culture she admires. Her drive to improve comes from the deep satisfaction she feels every time she learns something new.

Why It's Powerful: Intrinsic motivation is often more sustainable than extrinsic motivation. When you genuinely enjoy or value an activity, you're more likely to stick with it, even when progress is slow.

How to Foster Intrinsic Motivation:

- **Align Habits with Personal Values**: Choose goals that matter deeply to you. For instance, if you value creativity, commit to a daily sketching habit.

- **Find Joy in the Process**: Focus on the experience of doing the habit, not just the outcome. If you're learning guitar, enjoy the sound of the strings under your fingers, even before you can play full songs.

- **Challenge Yourself**: Intrinsic motivation thrives on a balance between effort and reward. Set goals that stretch you without overwhelming you.

Extrinsic Motivation: External Forces at Work

Extrinsic motivation, on the other hand, is driven by external factors, such as rewards, recognition, or the avoidance of negative consequences. It's the reason you might go to the gym to earn a fitness badge, meet a weight-loss goal, or avoid a stern lecture from your doctor.

For example, consider Jonathan, who started exercising because his company offered a bonus for employees who hit their wellness targets. Initially, the bonus was his sole motivator. But over time, as he began to enjoy the routine and notice improvements in his health, the activity became intrinsically rewarding.

Why It's Powerful: Extrinsic motivation is often effective for kick-starting habits, especially when intrinsic motivation hasn't developed yet. A tangible reward can provide the initial push needed to get started.

How to Leverage Extrinsic Motivation:

- **Set Clear Rewards**: Tie your habit to specific, meaningful rewards, like treating yourself to a movie night after a week of consistent workouts.

- **Use Social Accountability**: Commit to your habit publicly or join a group working toward similar goals. The desire to meet others' expectations can be a strong motivator.

- **Create Consequences**: Introduce stakes for not following through, such as donating to a cause you dislike if you skip a habit.

How Intrinsic and Extrinsic Motivation Work Together

One of the most effective ways to sustain habits is by blending intrinsic and extrinsic motivation. Start with extrinsic motivators to build momentum, then nurture intrinsic motivation as you begin to see the value or joy in the habit itself.

Leah, a florist, wanted to improve her photography skills to showcase her arrangements on social media. While she loved her work, taking photos felt like a chore—she had little experience and didn't enjoy fumbling with her camera. To jumpstart the habit, Leah joined an online photography course that awarded badges for completing assignments and allowed members to share their progress with the group.

At first, Leah was motivated by external rewards. She was determined to collect all the badges and enjoyed the praise she received from the group when she uploaded her photos. But as she practiced, she started noticing something unexpected: she began to enjoy the creative process of setting up her shots, playing with lighting, and finding the perfect angle.

What started as a way to earn badges and impress her peers became a personal passion. Leah found herself taking photos outside of her assignments, capturing flowers in her garden or street scenes that caught her eye. By the end of the course, Leah's motivation had shifted from extrinsic to intrinsic. Photography had become more than just a skill for her business—it was now a creative outlet that brought her joy.

What to Do When Motivation Wanes

Even with a deep understanding of motivation, there will be days when it feels absent.

Here's how to keep going when motivation dips:

- **Focus on Discipline**: Motivation might get you started, but discipline sustains you. Rely on systems, like habit stacking or accountability, to carry you through low-motivation days.

- **Reconnect with Your Why**: Remind yourself why the habit matters. Reflect on how it aligns with your goals or the benefits it's already brought to your life.

- **Embrace Small Wins**: Scale back the habit to its smallest version to maintain momentum. For example, if you're too tired for your full workout, do five minutes of stretching instead.

A Story of Motivation in Action

Lila, an artist and part-time teacher, wanted to build a habit of painting daily to prepare for an upcoming exhibition. Initially, she relied on extrinsic motivation—a promise to her mentor that she'd complete 30 paintings by the exhibition date. Each week, she updated her mentor on her progress, knowing that failing to deliver would be embarrassing.

As the weeks passed, Lila discovered something unexpected: she began to enjoy her daily painting sessions. The act of mixing colors, experimenting with techniques, and watching her canvases come to life became deeply fulfilling. By the time the exhibition arrived, she had far exceeded her goal, completing 45 paintings. Lila's habit started with external accountability but transformed into an intrinsic love for the craft.

Motivation is Dynamic, Not Static

Motivation isn't a constant force—it ebbs and flows, influenced by your circumstances, emotions, and environment. The key to sustaining habits is understanding how to harness both intrinsic and extrinsic motivators and knowing when to lean on one more heavily than the other.

When motivation feels strong, use it to push forward. When it's weak, rely on systems, discipline, and your understanding of why the habit matters. By recognizing the dynamic nature of motivation, you can navigate its fluctuations and continue making progress.

The 1% Rule

Change doesn't have to be dramatic to be meaningful. Often, the most profound transformations are rooted in tiny, consistent improvements. This is the essence of the 1% Rule: the idea that if you aim to improve by just 1% each day, the cumulative effect will be extraordinary.

A 1% improvement may sound trivial, but over time, it compounds. Think about compound interest in finance—small investments grow exponentially when given enough time. The same principle applies to habits. Each small action builds on the last, creating momentum that propels you toward your goals.

Why the 1% Rule Works

The genius of the 1% Rule lies in its simplicity. Big goals can feel overwhelming and unattainable, leading many to abandon them before they begin. By contrast, a 1% improvement feels manageable—achievable even on the toughest days.

Here's the math: improving by 1% every day for a year doesn't just lead to a 365% improvement—it's closer to 3,800% because of the power of compounding. This exponential growth shows how even the smallest actions can lead to monumental change over time.

The Snowball Effect of Small Improvements

Mia, a high school teacher, often felt like she was running on a treadmill set to max speed. Between grading, lesson planning, and managing extracurricular activities, her to-do list always seemed longer at the end of the day than at the start. She loved teaching, but the constant sense of being behind left her feeling overwhelmed and discouraged.

One afternoon, as she stared at the towering stack of ungraded essays on her desk, Mia stumbled upon an idea that sparked her curiosity: the 1% Rule. The concept was simple—focus on improving by just 1% each day, no grand leaps required. She decided to give it a try, setting aside just 10 minutes each day to tackle small, manageable tasks.

At first, the effort felt insignificant. What could 10 minutes accomplish when her workload seemed so endless? But Mia stuck with it. One day, she graded a handful of essays; the next, she outlined the introduction to a lesson plan. Slowly but surely, those short bursts of focused effort began to chip away at her backlog.

A surprising thing happened as the days turned into weeks: the momentum built on itself. Mia started noticing patterns in her workload and developed systems to streamline her tasks. She prioritized grading during her most focused hours and saved simpler tasks for moments when her energy waned. By the middle of the semester, she wasn't just caught up—she was ahead.

For the first time in years, Mia had room to breathe. With her newfound time, she began mentoring struggling students one-on-one and experimenting with more creative, engaging lesson plans. Her classroom became a space where both she and her students thrived.

The changes extended beyond her work. By reclaiming her evenings, Mia rediscovered time for herself—reading, reconnecting with friends, and even starting a yoga class. What began as a modest effort to tackle her workload had transformed not only her career but her sense of balance and fulfillment.

Today, Mia continues to embrace the 1% Rule. "It's not about doing everything all at once," she often tells her colleagues. "It's about showing up every day, even in small ways. The rest takes care of itself."

Take Darren, for instance—a father of two who spent most of his days sitting at a desk. His work as an accountant left little time for exercise, and by the end of the day, he often chose the couch and a TV remote over anything active. He wasn't looking to become an athlete; he just wanted to feel better and improve his health.

One day, after a routine check-up revealed rising blood pressure and borderline cholesterol issues, Darren realized he needed to make a change. The idea of starting a workout routine felt overwhelming—how could he possibly find the time or energy? So, he started with something so small it seemed almost laughable: running for one minute a day.

That first minute wasn't glamorous, but it was a step. The next day, he ran for two minutes. Then three. Within a few weeks, Darren found himself jogging around his neighborhood for 10 minutes each evening. It became a simple ritual—just him, his sneakers, and the fresh air.

After a few months, Darren started to feel different. His energy levels improved, and his stress seemed to melt away during those quiet runs. One evening, he thought to himself, *Why not sign up for a 5K?* It wasn't about being fast; it was about proving to himself that he could finish.

The 5K was a success. Darren crossed the finish line with a huge grin and a sense of accomplishment that lit a spark. From there, he gradually pushed himself further—training for a 10K, then a half marathon. Each step felt like a natural extension of the progress he'd already made.

Finally, Darren set his sights on the ultimate challenge: running a marathon. The training was grueling at times, but he leaned on the same principle that had carried him this far—the 1% Rule. Each week, he added a little more distance to his runs, never worrying about being perfect, just focused on steady improvement.

When Darren crossed the marathon finish line a year later, it wasn't just about completing the race. It was about the journey: how one small habit—running for a single minute—had snowballed into something life-changing. Darren didn't just feel healthier; he felt more confident, more resilient, and more connected to his family, who had cheered him on every step of the way.

Applying the 1% Rule in Everyday Life

The beauty of the 1% Rule is its versatility. It's not limited to athletic or professional goals—it works in any area of life.

- **Personal Growth:** Want to read more? Commit to reading one paragraph or one page a day. Over time, those small reading sessions add up to books devoured and insights gained.

- **Financial Habits:** Saving money doesn't have to mean drastic sacrifices. Start by setting aside 1% of your income each month. As it becomes second nature, increase the amount incrementally.

- **Health and Fitness:** Aiming for better health? Begin with a one-minute walk after meals or adding one vegetable to your daily diet.

The key is to make the process sustainable. Small improvements compound because they're easy to maintain, even when motivation wanes.

Overcoming the Impatience Trap

A common challenge with the 1% Rule is impatience. In a world that glorifies instant results, it's easy to feel like small changes aren't worth the effort. But remember, the power of compounding lies in its long-term impact.

Here's a metaphor to keep in mind: Planting a tree. At first, the growth is invisible—just a seed buried in the soil. But with consistent watering and sunlight, that seed gradually takes root.

Over time, it grows into a sapling, then a sturdy tree. The process is slow, but the reward is lasting. The same goes for the 1% Rule: small daily actions may seem insignificant, but with time, they build a strong foundation for success.

How to Get Started with the 1% Rule

To implement the 1% Rule effectively, follow these steps:

Identify Your Target Area: Decide where you want to see improvement—whether it's your career, health, relationships, or hobbies.

Set a Micro Goal: Break your target into the smallest, most manageable action possible.

Track Your Progress: Keep a log to see how each small step adds up over time. This visual cue reinforces the value of your efforts.

Celebrate Incremental Wins: Recognize the progress you've made, no matter how small. Small victories build confidence and keep you motivated.

A Life of Continuous Improvement

The 1% Rule isn't about perfection—it's about progress. It reminds us that big results don't come from giant leaps but from the steady accumulation of small wins. By focusing on incremental improvements, you're not just changing your habits—you're changing your trajectory.

What could you accomplish if you got 1% better each day? The answer lies in the tiny actions you take today and the consistency you bring to them tomorrow. Start small, stay steady, and watch as the power of compounding works its magic.

Habits and Decision Fatigue

Every day, we make hundreds of decisions. What to wear. What to eat. When to check email. Which tasks to tackle first. Individually, these decisions may seem trivial, but they accumulate, taxing our mental energy and leaving us drained. This phenomenon, known as decision fatigue, affects everyone, no matter how disciplined or focused you may be. It's why even the most productive people struggle to choose what's for dinner after a long day.

But here's the good news: habits can help. By automating certain behaviors, you reduce the number of decisions you need to make, preserving your mental energy for what truly matters. Simplifying your choices through habits isn't just practical; it's essential for long-term success and well-being. Habits don't just streamline your life; they create a foundation for clarity and intentionality in your daily actions.

The Hidden Cost of Decision Fatigue

Rachel's mornings always felt like a whirlwind. She'd stare at her closet, trying to piece together an outfit, only to realize she was running late. Breakfast became a rushed decision—should she grab a protein bar or cook eggs? By the time she sat down to work, her brain already felt cluttered, and it wasn't even 9 a.m. Yet Rachel couldn't understand why she was so exhausted by the end of the day, even before tackling her to-do list.

What Rachel didn't realize was that every choice she made, no matter how small, drained her mental resources. Decision fatigue isn't about making bad choices—it's about being overwhelmed by the sheer volume of decisions. Over time, this constant mental drain can erode your ability to maintain long-term habits and make thoughtful choices, leading to a cycle of reactive rather than proactive behavior. Left unchecked, decision fatigue can negatively impact well-being, increasing stress and diminishing your overall sense of control. And when mental energy runs low, the quality of our decisions tends to decline. It's why you might find yourself defaulting to fast food, skipping workouts, or procrastinating after a long day.

Decision fatigue doesn't just affect productivity; it can seep into emotional and social aspects of life. For example, constantly deciding between work obligations and personal commitments can lead to feelings of guilt or resentment. Over time, this emotional strain compounds, making it even harder to maintain a balanced and intentional life.

Habits as a Solution to Decision Fatigue

Habits are powerful because they take decisions off your plate. From a cognitive perspective, habits automate behavior by shifting tasks from the decision-heavy prefrontal cortex to the more efficient basal ganglia. This reduces the mental load associated with repetitive choices, freeing up cognitive resources for more complex or creative decisions. By tying this back to decision fatigue, we can see how cultivating habits acts as a mental energy-saving tool, allowing you to focus on what truly matters. When an action becomes automatic, you no longer have to deliberate about it. This frees up cognitive space for the decisions that truly matter.

Consider Paul, a graphic designer who struggled with procrastination. His mornings used to start with indecision: should he begin with client emails or dive into a project? By the time he chose, he'd already wasted valuable time. To simplify his mornings, Paul developed a habit: every workday, he spent the first 20 minutes organizing his tasks with a prioritized list. This routine eliminated the need to debate his starting point each day.

Over time, Paul noticed that his mornings felt calmer, and his productivity improved. By removing one decision from his routine, he had more energy to focus on creative work. This energy-saving effect rippled throughout his day, allowing him to approach complex projects with greater clarity and enthusiasm.

Habits don't just simplify your day—they act as anchors in a chaotic world. They provide a sense of stability, helping you navigate the unpredictability of life with greater ease and confidence.

The Power of Defaults

One of the simplest ways to combat decision fatigue is by setting defaults. Defaults are pre-made choices that guide your behavior without requiring conscious effort.

Take meal planning. Claire, a busy parent, used to agonize over what to cook each night. The stress of daily meal decisions led to frequent takeout orders. To reclaim her evenings, Claire adopted a default meal schedule: Mondays were pasta nights, Tuesdays were taco nights, and so on. This system didn't mean she always cooked the same dishes, but it gave her a starting point, reducing the mental load of deciding from scratch.

Defaults work because they narrow your options, making decisions easier. In professional settings, for instance, establishing a default meeting agenda can streamline preparation and ensure consistency across discussions. Similarly, pre-scheduling time for focused work eliminates the need to decide when to tackle critical tasks, keeping your day structured and efficient. Whether it's pre-selecting your outfits, scheduling workouts, or organizing your workday, defaults help you focus on execution rather than deliberation.

Imagine how much smoother your day could be if certain decisions were already made for you. For example, setting a default time for grocery shopping every week not only saves time but also ensures that healthier food options are always stocked. This seemingly small change can lead to long-term benefits in both health and productivity.

Creating Decision-Free Zones

Another strategy for minimizing decision fatigue is to create "decision-free zones" in your life—areas where habits and routines handle the bulk of your choices.

For example, Mary, a software developer, felt overwhelmed by the endless notifications and emails that filled her workday. She instituted a decision-free zone by designating specific times to check her email: once in the morning and once after lunch. During these windows, she processed her inbox fully, freeing herself from the constant "should I check now?" debate.

Similarly, you might create a decision-free morning routine. Lay out your clothes the night before, prepare breakfast in advance, or follow a consistent workout schedule. By automating these parts of your day, you preserve your mental energy for more meaningful tasks.

Decision-free zones can also extend to your digital life. Consider disabling non-essential notifications on your devices or using website blockers during work hours. These small actions create mental boundaries, reducing the cognitive load of constant interruptions.

Small Choices, Big Impact

Sometimes, the smallest habits can have the biggest impact on reducing decision fatigue. Think about how much time and energy you spend deciding what to wear. Many high-performing individuals, like Steve Jobs and Barack Obama, famously limited their wardrobes to reduce decision-making. You don't need to adopt a uniform, but simplifying your options—such as sticking to a color palette or planning outfits weekly—can save valuable mental energy.

Similarly, automating financial decisions can alleviate stress. Just as Claire's meal planning streamlined her evenings, automating financial tasks removes the constant mental juggling of bills and savings. This universal principle—letting systems handle recurring choices—frees your mind to focus on more rewarding pursuits. Direct deposits into savings accounts, scheduled bill payments, and pre-set budgets remove the need for constant financial deliberation. These small steps free up your focus for larger goals.

Beyond finances and meals, small changes like setting a default bedtime or automating weekly chore schedules can have outsized effects. These habits create a foundation for balance, allowing you to channel your energy into areas that truly matter.

The Ripple Effect of Simplified Choices

When you reduce decision fatigue in one area of your life, the benefits often extend to others. For example, simplifying your workday routines can free up energy for creative hobbies in the evening or allow for more quality time with loved ones. This interconnected effect highlights how seemingly small changes can create balance and clarity across multiple aspects of your life. For instance, Megan, a teacher, used to feel paralyzed by her endless to-do list. She started small, creating a habit of prioritizing three tasks each morning. This simple change didn't just streamline her workday—it gave her more energy to spend time with her kids and pursue hobbies in the evenings. Simplifying her choices created a ripple effect of calm and clarity across her life.

The same principle applies to your habits. Automating your meals, workouts, or daily routines doesn't just save time—it strengthens your ability to tackle bigger challenges with focus and energy. These ripples often inspire others around you, creating a culture of intentional living within your family or workplace.

Building Your Decision-Simplifying System

To make habits work for you, start by identifying the areas where decision fatigue hits hardest. Is it your mornings? Your meals? Your work schedule? Once you've pinpointed the problem, create a system that automates or simplifies those choices.

1. **Choose One Area to Focus On:** Start with the part of your day that feels most chaotic.

2. **Set Defaults:** Establish go-to routines or options, like a regular breakfast or a weekly workout schedule.

3. **Create Habits to Eliminate Repetition:** Look for recurring decisions you can automate, like prepping meals in advance or setting reminders for tasks.

4. **Reflect and Adjust:** As your routines evolve, make tweaks to ensure they're still serving you.

Experiment with different approaches and refine your system over time. The goal is not to eliminate spontaneity but to create a structure that supports your priorities and well-being.

The Gift of Mental Energy

Every decision you automate through habits is a gift of mental energy to yourself. By reducing decision fatigue, you free your mind to focus on what truly matters—whether it's pursuing your passions, spending time with loved ones, or excelling in your career. Habits don't just simplify your life; they empower you to use your energy where it counts most.

Simplifying your choices through habits isn't about removing spontaneity. It's about creating the mental space to embrace the moments that matter, unburdened by unnecessary deliberation. So, as you look at your daily routines, ask yourself: what decisions can I let my habits take care of? Then watch as your newfound clarity transforms not just your day, but your life.

By cultivating habits that reduce decision fatigue, you're not just organizing your day—you're reclaiming your mental bandwidth, energy, and focus for the things that make life meaningful. Small adjustments in how you approach decisions can lead to profound transformations, leaving you feeling more in control and capable of achieving your goals.

The Ripple Effect

Have you ever tossed a pebble into a still pond and watched the ripples spread outward? That's the ripple effect—a single action creating waves that travel far beyond the point of impact. When applied to habits, it's the idea that a small, positive change in one area of life can spark a chain reaction of benefits in others.

While the 1% Rule focuses on incremental improvement, the ripple effect takes it a step further, showing how those improvements can multiply across different aspects of your life. Think of it as compounding, but not just within a single habit—it radiates outward, enhancing your well-being, relationships, and opportunities.

How the Ripple Effect Works

Habits are rarely isolated. Instead, they're deeply interconnected, like the strands of a web. When you strengthen one part of the web, the entire structure becomes more resilient. This is the ripple effect in action: small changes you make in one area often create unexpected and far-reaching improvements in others.

For example, starting a habit of daily exercise might seem like it's only about physical health. But soon, you might notice that you're sleeping better, handling stress more effectively, and even making healthier food choices. A single habit—consistent exercise—ripples outward, creating a cascade of positive changes.

Real-World Stories of the Ripple Effect

Priya, a graduate student pursuing a demanding program, often felt like she was drowning in responsibilities. Deadlines loomed like storm clouds, and her mind buzzed with a constant swirl of to-dos. Despite her best efforts to stay on top of her coursework, she struggled to focus and frequently found herself scrambling to finish assignments at the last minute.

One particularly stressful evening, Priya stumbled across an article about the power of journaling. The idea intrigued her—could writing her thoughts down really make a difference? She decided to give it a try, setting aside just five minutes each morning to jot down her thoughts and outline her priorities for the day.

At first, the habit felt awkward. Priya wasn't used to slowing down, and the blank page seemed almost intimidating. But she persisted, scribbling whatever came to mind: tasks she needed to tackle, worries that had been keeping her up at night, and even small moments of gratitude.

Over the weeks, something shifted. Those five quiet minutes at the start of her day began to act as a reset button for her overwhelmed mind. Writing her thoughts down brought clarity, helping her identify what truly mattered and let go of what didn't. The act of journaling became a space for her to breathe, reflect, and recalibrate.

As her sense of control grew, so did her productivity. Priya found it easier to break assignments into manageable steps, and for the first time in her academic career, she began submitting work ahead of schedule. The nagging anxiety that had plagued her for months started to fade, replaced by a steady confidence in her ability to handle her workload.

But the benefits didn't stop there. With her schedule more organized and her mind less cluttered, Priya found herself with time and energy to spare. She began revisiting hobbies she had abandoned during the chaos of her program—painting, practicing yoga, and even taking weekend walks in the park. These small joys reminded her of who she was beyond her studies, adding a sense of balance and fulfillment to her life.

By the end of the semester, Priya couldn't believe how far she'd come. What had started as a simple experiment to reduce stress had blossomed into a habit that touched every part of her life. Journaling wasn't just a productivity tool—it was a lifeline, a reminder that even in the busiest seasons, taking time for yourself can create ripple effects of clarity, calm, and connection.

Today, Priya's journal is never far from her side. She still spends a few minutes each morning writing, knowing that those small moments hold the power to transform her day—and her life.

Leo, a sales manager whose days were a constant whirlwind of meetings, calls, and deadlines. His role demanded energy and sharp thinking, but by mid-afternoon, he often found himself hitting a wall. He'd reach for snacks or another cup of coffee to power through, but it never really helped. The problem wasn't his workload—it was his posture. Hours of slouching at his desk left him with aching shoulders, tension headaches, and a sense of physical fatigue that sapped his mental focus.

One day, while scrolling through an article on wellness, Leo stumbled upon a simple tip: incorporate regular stretching into your workday. It wasn't flashy or time-intensive, but the idea of feeling better physically intrigued him. He decided to give it a shot, starting with something small: standing up and stretching his shoulders for just 30 seconds each time he finished a call.

At first, it felt odd—interrupting his momentum to stretch didn't come naturally. But within days, Leo noticed a difference. Those brief pauses didn't just loosen his shoulders; they cleared his mind, too. The stretches became a moment to reset, both physically and mentally, allowing him to approach his next task with renewed focus.

Encouraged by the results, Leo expanded his routine, adding neck rolls and quick back stretches to the mix. By the end of the month, the tension headaches he'd grown so used to were almost nonexistent, and his energy levels stayed steady throughout the day.

As the weeks went on, Leo found unexpected benefits. His brief stretches sparked conversations with coworkers who noticed him standing and moving around more. "What's your secret?" they'd ask, curious about his newfound energy. Stretching had gone from a solitary habit to a shared office culture, with colleagues joining him during breaks.

Six months later, Leo had turned his small habit into a comprehensive routine. He started each morning with a few minutes of stretching to set the tone for his day, incorporated mobility exercises during lunch breaks, and ended his evenings with a calming stretch to wind down. The benefits weren't just physical—Leo's productivity soared, and his stress levels plummeted. He even inspired his team to adopt similar habits, fostering a healthier, more connected work environment.

What began as a modest experiment to relieve tension transformed Leo's approach to his workday and his well-being. Today, he's a firm believer in the power of small physical changes to unlock big results. "Sometimes," he says, "it's not about working harder—it's about taking care of yourself in the moments that matter most."

Why the Ripple Effect is Powerful

The ripple effect is so powerful because it's not linear—it's exponential. One good habit can create an ecosystem of benefits, with each improvement reinforcing and amplifying the others.

For example:

- Adopting a regular sleep schedule might lead to better mood regulation, which strengthens relationships and improves decision-making at work.

- Starting a gratitude practice could help you reframe challenges, leading to greater resilience and a more positive outlook on life.

- Learning a new skill might boost your confidence, opening doors to opportunities you never thought possible.

Small changes don't just stay small. They create waves that touch every part of your life, often in ways you didn't anticipate.

The Ripple Effect vs. The 1% Rule

It's important to distinguish the ripple effect from the 1% Rule. While both emphasize small, consistent actions, they operate differently.

- **The 1% Rule** is about steady, incremental improvement within a specific habit or skill. It's the disciplined path of getting a little better every day.

- **The Ripple Effect** is about the interconnectedness of habits and how improvements in one area can cascade into others, creating a broader transformation.

Together, they form a powerful duo: the 1% Rule builds momentum, and the ripple effect amplifies its impact across your life.

How to Create Your Own Ripple Effect

1. **Start with One Habit**: Choose a small, meaningful habit that aligns with your goals. For example, if you want to improve your energy levels, commit to stretching for five minutes each morning.

2. **Observe the Changes**: Pay attention to how this habit affects other areas of your life. Are you feeling more focused? Making better decisions?

3. **Build on Momentum**: Once you notice the ripples, use that energy to reinforce or expand your habits. For in-

stance, stretching in the morning could lead to incorporating a short workout or mindfulness practice.

4. **Reflect and Adjust**: Periodically evaluate your habits and their broader impact. What's working well? What could you tweak to create even bigger ripples?

The ripple effect reminds us that no action is too small to matter. Every choice we make has the potential to create waves, influencing our lives in ways we might not immediately see. By embracing this principle, you're not just building better habits—you're setting the stage for a life filled with interconnected growth and transformation.

What's one habit you can start today that might create ripples in your own life? The answer could be simpler—and more impactful—than you think.

Seasonal Habits and the Rhythms of Life

Life is inherently cyclical. The seasons change, the days lengthen and shorten, and our energy ebbs and flows along with these natural rhythms. Yet, we often expect ourselves to maintain a steady, unchanging pace throughout the year. This disconnect can lead to frustration, burnout, and missed opportunities to align our habits with the environment around us. Embracing seasonal habits—habits that shift and adapt with the seasons—offers a way to work with nature, rather than against it.

Seasonal habits allow us to harness the unique opportunities and challenges of each time of year. While opportunities might include the energy of spring renewal or the abundance of summer, challenges can arise from the slower pace of winter or the busyness of fall transitions. By addressing these seasonal challenges head-on, such as combating winter blues with mindful rest or managing fall's demands with better planning, seasonal habits become tools for balance and resilience. They encourage flexibility and mindfulness, helping us align our routines with the rhythms of life. By integrating these habits, we can cultivate a deeper connection to ourselves and the world around us.

The Wisdom of Seasonal Living

For centuries, humans lived in sync with the seasons. Farmers planted in spring, harvested in summer and fall, and rested during the quiet months of winter. These cycles weren't just practical—they shaped the way people ate, worked, and rested. Modern life, with its artificial lights and year-round schedules, has largely disconnected us from these rhythms. But the wisdom of seasonal living still holds value.

Take Lena, an artist who felt uninspired during the gray months of winter. Instead of forcing herself to maintain her usual pace, she decided to lean into the season. She established a winter habit of reflection, spending 15 minutes each evening journaling about her day. The habit wasn't about producing anything tangible; it was about embracing the slower, introspective energy of winter. When spring arrived, Lena transitioned to an active habit: a morning walk to observe the new growth around her. These seasonal shifts not only matched her natural energy levels but also deepened her creative wellspring.

Seasonal habits don't mean overhauling your routines every three months. Instead, they invite you to ask: How can I align my habits with the energy of this season? What opportunities does this time of year offer? The answers often lead to habits that feel more natural and sustainable, rather than forced.

Spring: Growth and Renewal

Spring is a time of new beginnings, when nature bursts back to life. For instance, someone might use this season's sense of renewal to revisit a neglected goal, such as completing a half-finished novel or restarting a fitness routine. The fresh energy of spring often makes it easier to re-engage with projects that felt stagnant during the colder months. The longer days and warmer weather often bring a surge of energy and optimism. It's the perfect season to plant the seeds of new habits and let them take root.

For example, you might use spring as a time to begin an outdoor exercise routine, like running, biking, or gardening. The act of being outside not only enhances physical health but also connects you to the vibrancy of the season. Alternatively, spring can be a time to declutter your physical and mental spaces, making room for growth and creativity. This season is also ideal for revisiting goals that may have gone dormant during winter.

Habits to consider in spring:

- Starting a gratitude journal to reflect on the new opportunities around you.
- Tackling a creative project that excites you.
- Spending time in nature to recharge and refocus.
- Reviving a neglected hobby or skill that aligns with the season's energy.

Spring's sense of renewal makes it a natural time to reassess your routines and experiment with new habits, such as outdoor creative projects or decluttering. This season provides the energy to break free from winter's inertia and embrace growth.

Summer: Energy and Connection

Summer's long, sunny days are filled with opportunities for connection, adventure, and celebration. This is a season to embrace habits that energize you and strengthen your relationships. The abundance of daylight and warmth often inspires outdoor activities and social gatherings, making it a time to build habits that bring joy and connection.

Elliot, a teacher, made a summer habit of weekly picnics with friends and family. It was a simple way to unwind, strengthen his social bonds, and savor the season's abundance. For others, summer might be the ideal time to take on an ambitious fitness goal, join a community class, or explore new hobbies that thrive in the sun.

Habits to consider in summer:

- Planning weekly outdoor activities to stay active and engaged.

- Establishing a habit of weekend adventures, like hiking or visiting local attractions.

- Practicing mindfulness through seasonal rituals, like watching the sunrise or tending a garden.

- Exploring creative pursuits, such as photography or painting, inspired by the vibrant landscapes of summer.

Summer also encourages spontaneity. Building flexible habits that allow for impromptu moments of joy—like a last-minute trip to the beach—can make the season feel even more fulfilling.

Fall: Reflection and Preparation

Fall, with its transitional energy, naturally supports reflection and purposeful planning. Aligning with this seasonal rhythm allows you to focus on organization, learning, and gratitude in a way that feels intuitive rather than forced. It's a time to gather the fruits of your efforts, both literally and metaphorically, and reflect on what you've accomplished. Just as farmers harvest their crops, fall invites us to acknowledge our personal achievements and consider how they prepare us for the future. This reflection can fuel a sense of gratitude and provide clarity for setting new intentions.

Cecelia, a small business owner, used fall to review her professional goals. She developed a habit of dedicating one evening a week to strategic planning, reflecting on her successes and identifying areas for improvement. This practice not only helped her achieve clarity but also allowed her to set realistic intentions for the coming year.

Habits to consider in fall:

- Reviewing and revising your long-term goals.
- Taking a class or learning a new skill to prepare for future challenges.
- Creating a gratitude practice to appreciate the year's experiences.

- Organizing your home or workspace to reflect the season's spirit of preparation.

Fall is also a season of harvest—both literally and metaphorically. It's a time to celebrate the fruits of your labor and to use those reflections as fuel for future growth. By embracing this sense of culmination, fall becomes a powerful time to recalibrate and lay the groundwork for the seasons ahead.

Winter: Rest and Renewal

Winter's slower pace encourages deeper connections and introspection. It's an ideal time to nurture relationships through small, meaningful rituals, like family game nights or cozy meals, while also prioritizing self-care through reflective habits. It's a season for rest, reflection, and renewal—an opportunity to embrace habits that nurture your mind and body. The shorter days and colder weather naturally encourage more time indoors, making this an ideal season for quiet, restorative practices.

For Nathan, a busy executive, winter became a season of self-care. He created a habit of winding down each evening with a cup of tea and a book, allowing himself to disconnect from work and recharge. This small but meaningful ritual helped him combat seasonal stress and enter the spring feeling refreshed.

Habits to consider in winter:

- Establishing a bedtime routine to improve sleep quality.
- Practicing daily mindfulness or meditation to combat seasonal blues.

- Engaging in creative hobbies, like writing, painting, or cooking, to nourish your spirit.
- Exploring reflective practices, such as journaling or vision boarding, to set the stage for the year ahead.

Winter is also a time to honor rest without guilt. By leaning into this slower energy, you create space to recharge fully, emerging into spring with renewed vitality and a clear sense of purpose.

Embracing Seasonal Rhythms

Seasonal habits remind us to flow with life's natural cycles, embracing periods of growth, rest, and renewal. This alignment not only enhances well-being and productivity but also deepens your connection to the world around you, turning each season into an opportunity for intentional living.

Ask yourself: What does this season invite me to focus on? Try journaling about the changes you notice in your energy, priorities, or surroundings. For example, you might list three things that feel more aligned with the season or write down one habit you'd like to adjust to better suit the time of year. Reflecting on these prompts can help you identify meaningful ways to adapt your routines. By embracing seasonal rhythms, you'll cultivate habits that not only enrich your life but also honor the beautiful, ever-changing cycles of nature.

Embracing these rhythms is more than just a practice—it's a mindset. It allows you to live in harmony with the world, celebrating each season for what it uniquely offers while finding balance and meaning throughout the year.

Habit Stacking

Building habits isn't just about adding new actions to your day; it's about integrating them into the life you already have. That's the genius of habit stacking—a strategy that leverages your existing routines as anchors for new habits, making them almost automatic.

Habit stacking is where practicality meets momentum. It takes the incremental progress of the 1% Rule and the cascading benefits of the Ripple Effect and turns them into an actionable framework. By connecting new habits to ones you're already doing, you reduce the mental effort required to remember, initiate, and maintain them.

What is Habit Stacking?

The concept is simple: you take an existing habit—something you already do regularly—and stack a new habit on top of it. The existing habit serves as a trigger, reminding you to perform the new one.

For example, if you already brush your teeth every morning, you could stack a habit of doing 10 squats immediately afterward.

Over time, this pairing becomes a seamless part of your routine, requiring little thought or effort.

Why Habit Stacking Works

Habit stacking works because it leverages the brain's natural tendency to link behaviors into patterns. It reduces decision fatigue by tying your new habit to an already established cue, and it creates a chain reaction of productivity and growth.

Unlike starting from scratch, habit stacking builds on routines you've already mastered, which means you're not creating an entirely new pathway—you're extending an existing one.

Real-World Examples of Habit Stacking

Carlos was a busy entrepreneur who wore many hats—CEO, marketer, problem-solver, and occasionally, office handyman. His days were a blur of meetings, emails, and urgent decisions, leaving him mentally drained by mid-afternoon. While he loved the thrill of running his own business, Carlos couldn't ignore the mounting stress that often left him feeling scattered and unfocused.

One evening, as he scrolled through a productivity blog, he came across the idea of mindful pauses: taking intentional moments throughout the day to reflect and reset. The concept intrigued him, but carving out extra time felt impossible. Instead, he decided to experiment by incorporating a simple habit into something he was already doing—his coffee breaks.

The next morning, Carlos made a subtle change. As his coffee brewed, instead of checking his email or reviewing his calendar, he leaned against the counter, closed his eyes, and spent two minutes asking himself a single question: *What's the one thing I need to accomplish today to make it a success?*

The first few days felt awkward. He'd catch himself reaching for his phone or letting his mind wander. But by the end of the week, something clicked. Those two minutes of focused reflection gave him clarity and purpose, helping him prioritize his most important tasks instead of getting lost in the day's chaos.

Encouraged by the results, Carlos stuck with the habit. Over the weeks, it became his favorite part of the morning—a quiet ritual that not only reduced his stress but sharpened his decision-making. He began noticing patterns in what he identified as priorities, which helped him delegate more effectively and plan his days with intention.

As his business grew, so did the impact of his habit. Employees began noticing how calm and clear-headed Carlos seemed during high-pressure situations. When they asked how he managed it, he shared his practice of mindful prioritization. Inspired, his team started adopting their own versions of his morning ritual, creating a ripple effect of focus and intentionality across the company.

A year later, Carlos reflected on how much his small habit had transformed his life. What started as a simple question over coffee had become the foundation for his success—not just as an entrepreneur but as a leader. His mornings were no longer chaotic but purposeful, and his sense of control extended far beyond the boardroom.

Today, Carlos continues his ritual, reminding himself that clarity doesn't require hours of effort—it starts with a single focused moment.

Bethany, a new mom, was still adjusting to the whirlwind of life with an infant. Her days were consumed with feedings, diaper changes, and endless rounds of cleaning bottles. Amidst the exhaustion and joy, she noticed something else—her body didn't feel like her own anymore. Activities that once came easily, like walking up stairs or carrying groceries, now left her feeling weak and winded. She wanted to regain her strength, but between her baby's unpredictable schedule and her own fatigue, finding time to exercise felt impossible.

One evening, as Bethany stood at the sink scrubbing bottles, she had an idea: *What if I used this time for something more?* It wasn't realistic to hit the gym or follow a structured workout, but she could at least move her body. She decided to start small, doing a quick set of calf raises every time she washed bottles.

The first time she tried it, she felt a bit silly, rising onto her toes while balancing a soapy bottle in one hand. But the movement was easy enough, and before long, it became second nature. Each time she stood at the sink, her body seemed to cue her: *It's time to move.*

Over the weeks, Bethany began to notice subtle changes. Her legs felt stronger, and her energy improved. Washing bottles no longer felt like a chore—it was a chance to sneak in a little time for herself. Encouraged, she added more movements to her routine: squats while waiting for the kettle to boil, arm circles while soothing her baby.

These micro moments of activity didn't just strengthen Bethany's body; they transformed her mindset. Instead of feeling stuck in the demands of motherhood, she started to see opportunities for growth and movement in the smallest pockets of her day.

As the months went on, Bethany's confidence grew. She began looking forward to her little "workouts" at the sink, knowing that each small action was a step toward reclaiming her strength. Her baby often watched from a nearby high chair, giggling as Bethany counted out her reps, making the routine a shared moment of connection.

By the end of the year, Bethany had built a surprising level of fitness without ever stepping foot in a gym. What started as a set of calf raises became a daily practice of finding joy and movement in her busy life. For Bethany, the habit wasn't just about exercise—it was about proving to herself that even in the chaos of motherhood, she could prioritize her well-being.

Today, Bethany encourages other new moms to find their own small ways to move, reminding them that strength isn't built all at once—it's created in the little moments that add up.

The Key to Successful Habit Stacking

The success of habit stacking lies in its simplicity and alignment with your existing life.

Follow these steps to create your own habit stack:

1. **Identify Your Anchor Habit:** Look for something you already do daily and consistently, such as brushing your teeth, brewing coffee, or starting your car.

2. **Choose a New Habit:** Pick a habit that's small and specific. For example, if you want to drink more water, commit to drinking a glass immediately after brushing your teeth.

3. **Pair Them Together:** Write it out as an "if-then" statement. For example: "If I brew coffee in the morning, then I will do two minutes of stretching."

4. **Start Small:** Avoid overloading your stack. Begin with one or two habits and let them solidify before adding more.

5. **Track Your Progress:** Use a habit tracker or journal to ensure consistency and celebrate milestones along the way.

Building a Chain Reaction with Habit Stacking

The beauty of habit stacking is its potential to create a chain reaction of positive behaviors. When stacked habits work together, they amplify the Ripple Effect, improving multiple areas of life.

For instance, someone who stacks drinking water after brushing their teeth might notice they feel more hydrated and energized, which leads to healthier food choices and improved concentration at work. These secondary benefits create a cycle of reinforcement, making the original habit even more valuable.

Customizing Habit Stacks to Your Goals

Habit stacking is endlessly adaptable.

Here are examples tailored to different goals:

- **Fitness:** After taking off your work shoes, change into workout clothes to cue an evening exercise routine.
- **Productivity:** When you sit down at your desk, write your top three priorities for the day before opening emails.
- **Mindfulness:** While waiting for your morning coffee, practice gratitude by jotting down three things you're thankful for.
- **Parenting:** After reading your child a bedtime story, spend five minutes reflecting on your parenting wins for the day.

Common Pitfalls and How to Avoid Them

While habit stacking is straightforward, it's not without challenges.

Here's how to overcome common obstacles:

- **Overloading Your Stack:** Adding too many habits at once can overwhelm you. Stick to one or two habits until they feel automatic.
- **Choosing Weak Anchors:** Ensure your anchor habit is consistent. A habit you only do sporadically won't be a reliable trigger.
- **Neglecting Flexibility:** Life happens, and routines shift. Be willing to adapt your habit stack as needed to stay

consistent.

Harnessing the Power of Habit Stacking

Habit stacking isn't just a strategy; it's a superpower for creating a life that aligns with your goals. By attaching new habits to the foundation of your existing routines, you make growth inevitable.

What new habit could you stack onto something you already do? Start small, stay consistent, and let the stacks build your pathway to success.

Tracking Progress and Staying Motivated

Tracking Progress and Staying Motivated

Imagine you're climbing a mountain. The summit looms large in your mind, a mix of excitement and doubt tugging at your thoughts. But as you take each step, something remarkable happens. You begin to notice the beauty along the way—the wildflowers lining the trail, the refreshing breeze, the small milestones you pass. Tracking your progress is like pausing to notice these moments on your journey. It grounds you in the present and reminds you how far you've come.

In habit formation, progress tracking serves as both a guide and a motivator. It shows you the path ahead while affirming that the steps you've already taken matter. Alongside this, celebrating wins keeps your spirit alive, giving you the fuel to keep climbing even when the trail feels steep.

Why Progress Tracking Transforms Habits

The process of tracking is deceptively simple. At its core, it's just a record of what you've done. But its impact on your brain—and your motivation—is profound. Each time you mark progress, whether it's a checkmark on a calendar or a streak on an app, your brain experiences a small hit of dopamine. This surge creates a positive association with the habit, encouraging you to repeat it.

But tracking does more than reinforce the behavior. It creates a sense of momentum. Humans are naturally drawn to patterns of growth, even in the smallest increments. Seeing evidence of consistency builds confidence, shifting your focus from *how far you have to go* to *how far you've come*.

Olivia, a busy mom juggling the needs of her family and a part-time job, often found herself feeling scattered and frazzled by mid-morning. The demands of her day left little room for focus, and by the time she sat down to tackle her work, her thoughts were already spinning with unfinished tasks and lingering stress.

One evening, she stumbled upon an idea while flipping through her planner: *What if I tracked my wins instead of my to-dos?* The thought intrigued her. She realized she spent her time chasing tasks but rarely acknowledged the things she accomplished. What if she made space to focus on the positives in her day?

The next morning, Olivia started a simple habit. Before diving into her work, she opened her planner and wrote down one small success from the day so far—anything from making breakfast on time to remembering to pack her child's homework. She called it her "win of the morning."

At first, it felt odd. The "wins" she wrote seemed trivial, like "loaded the dishwasher" or "took the kids to school without forgetting lunchboxes." But after a week, something shifted. Seeing her wins accumulate in her planner gave her a sense of momentum. Instead of focusing on what she hadn't done, she started the day feeling capable and accomplished.

As the weeks went on, Olivia's habit evolved. She began using her wins as fuel for her day. If she'd written down "stuck to a 10-minute chore schedule," she'd tackle her next task with confidence. By focusing on what she was doing *right*, Olivia found herself feeling more focused, energized, and in control.

Her new mindset began to ripple through her family. Her kids noticed the shift and started celebrating their own small wins—like setting the table or finishing homework without being reminded. The habit that had started as a personal exercise became a source of positivity and encouragement for her household.

Months later, Olivia looked back at her planner, filled with daily reminders of her progress. What had started as a small effort to regain focus had become a cornerstone of her day. For Olivia, tracking her wins wasn't just about feeling productive—it was about seeing herself as someone who could handle life's chaos with grace and confidence.

Today, Olivia still begins her mornings with her planner, logging her first win of the day. It's a habit that reminds her that no matter how overwhelming life feels, there's always something to celebrate—and that every small success adds up to something bigger.

Making Tracking Work for You

There's no one-size-fits-all method for tracking. Some people thrive on digital apps that send reminders and tally streaks, while others prefer the tactile satisfaction of checking off a box on paper. The magic lies not in the method but in the act of paying attention to your habits.

Progress tracking works because it aligns with how our brains process effort and reward. It takes the abstract—like "I want to write more"—and makes it concrete: "Today, I wrote 200 words." The key is to find a system that feels natural, not burdensome. The simpler the system, the more likely you are to stick with it.

For instance, Aaron, a high school teacher juggling grading and lesson plans, struggled to stay active. He started tracking his walking habit using a pedometer. Each evening, he reviewed his steps for the day. On low-step days, he'd reflect: Was I too busy? Did I forget to schedule a break? The pedometer didn't just count steps—it gave Aaron the clarity to adjust his habits and make walking a consistent part of his life.

Celebrating Wins: The Fuel for Consistency

Imagine running a marathon where no one cheers for you along the way, and there's no tape to break at the finish line. It would feel endless, draining your motivation long before you reached your goal. This is what habit formation looks like without celebration. Wins, no matter how small, give you those much-needed moments of recognition that make the effort feel worthwhile.

Celebrating wins isn't about inflating your ego or indulging unnecessarily. It's about reinforcing the link between effort and reward. When you celebrate, you tell your brain, "This matters. Keep going." Over time, these small acknowledgments add up, creating a positive emotional connection to the habit.

Anika, a graduate student immersed in the daunting task of writing her thesis. The project felt colossal, an Everest of research and writing that left her overwhelmed each time she sat at her desk. She knew her topic inside and out, but the sheer scale of the work ahead often paralyzed her.

After weeks of spinning her wheels, Anika decided to take a new approach. Instead of focusing on the mountain, she committed to taking one step at a time. Her plan was simple: write for just 30 minutes a day. It didn't matter if it was a full paragraph, a single sentence, or just revising a page—what mattered was showing up consistently.

To motivate herself, Anika paired the habit with something she loved: walking in the park near her campus. Each time she finished her 30-minute writing session, she laced up her shoes and headed outside. The fresh air and quiet surroundings felt like a reward, a way to clear her mind and celebrate her small victories.

At first, her progress was slow—just a few sentences here and there. But as the days turned into weeks, Anika began to notice a shift. The 30-minute sessions didn't feel so overwhelming anymore, and she found herself looking forward to her walks, which had become a treasured part of her routine.

The habit did more than keep her writing—it kept her grounded. The walks provided a chance to process her thoughts, brainstorm ideas, and reconnect with the joy of learning that had brought her to graduate school in the first place.

By the time Anika completed her thesis, she was stunned by how much she'd accomplished. What had once felt insurmountable had been tackled step by step, thanks to her daily commitment. Looking back, Anika realized it wasn't just the writing sessions that had carried her through—it was the habit of celebrating her consistency, one walk at a time.

Today, Anika continues to embrace the power of small habits paired with meaningful rewards. Whether it's a professional project or a personal goal, she knows the secret to progress isn't perfection—it's showing up, celebrating the effort, and letting each step build on the last.

The Feedback Loop of Progress and Motivation

Tracking and celebrating aren't just independent strategies; they amplify each other, creating a feedback loop that drives sustained motivation. Every time you track your progress, you reinforce your sense of accomplishment. Every celebration strengthens the emotional reward of sticking to your habit.

But what happens when motivation fades? This feedback loop is especially powerful during the inevitable dips in enthusiasm. Instead of relying on willpower alone, your progress becomes its own motivator. Each tracked day, each celebrated win is a reminder of the effort you've already invested—a nudge to keep going.

For example, Daniel, a novice painter, committed to practicing for 15 minutes daily. At first, his excitement carried him, but after a few weeks, the novelty wore off. On those tougher days, he'd look at his tracker, now filled with weeks of consistent practice. "I've come this far," he'd remind himself. That visible evidence, coupled with the joy he felt after finishing a painting session, kept him going until his habit became second nature.

Avoiding Perfectionism in Progress Tracking

It's easy to fall into the trap of thinking you need a perfect streak to succeed. But habits are not about perfection—they're about persistence. Missing a day doesn't erase your progress; it's an opportunity to learn and adjust.

Think of Mia, who was building a journaling habit. She missed a few days during a particularly hectic week and started to feel like she'd failed. But instead of abandoning her habit, she decided to treat those missed days as data. Why had she skipped? How could she plan differently? By shifting her mindset from perfectionism to curiosity, Mia not only got back on track but also refined her approach to make journaling more sustainable.

Rekindling Motivation Through Reflection

When progress feels slow, it's tempting to quit. But often, the antidote to waning motivation lies in reflection. Take time to revisit your "why." Why did you start this habit? What were you hoping to achieve? Sometimes, reconnecting with your deeper purpose can reignite your drive.

Reflection doesn't have to be complicated.

It can be as simple as asking yourself three questions at the end of each week:

- What went well?

- What could I improve?

- What's one thing I'm proud of?

These questions shift your focus from what's missing to what's possible, helping you see progress even when it feels incremental.

The Journey of Progress

Tracking your progress and celebrating your wins are more than tools—they're companions on your journey. They keep you grounded in the present while pulling you toward the future, reminding you that each step matters.

Whether it's the act of marking a day on a calendar, reflecting on a week's effort, or simply smiling at the end of a hard-fought workout, these small rituals create a steady rhythm that carries you forward. Habits aren't built in a day—but with progress and motivation as your guide, you'll reach heights you never thought possible.

Overcoming Obstacles

Every journey to self-improvement comes with its share of roadblocks. Some days, it feels like the wind is at your back, and progress is effortless. Other days, the path seems steep, and the motivation that once carried you falters.

Obstacles in habit-building aren't just likely—they're inevitable. Yet, they're not the end of the road. Instead, they're opportunities to adapt, grow, and prove to yourself that change is possible, even when it's difficult.

The Nature of Obstacles

Obstacles come in many forms. Sometimes they're external, like an unexpected deadline at work or a family emergency that derails your routine. Other times, they're internal, like a loss of motivation or the creeping perfectionism that whispers, *If you can't do it perfectly, why bother at all?*

These challenges are part of the process, not a detour from it. When you approach them with curiosity instead of frustration, you can uncover strategies that make you stronger. The key isn't to avoid obstacles—it's to navigate them with resilience.

Natalie, a mother of three, had always found cooking to be her creative escape. Preparing new recipes gave her a sense of calm and joy amidst the chaos of family life. But as her children's extracurricular schedules ramped up, evenings became a whirlwind of homework, carpooling, and rushed meals. Her once-beloved time in the kitchen dwindled to reheating leftovers and throwing together quick fixes.

For weeks, Natalie felt the loss acutely. Cooking had been her outlet, her way to unwind and express herself, and its absence left her feeling drained and disconnected. Guilt crept in—she couldn't find the time to cook the elaborate meals she loved, so she told herself there was no point in trying at all.

But instead of giving up, Natalie decided to adapt. Rather than aiming for elaborate recipes, she focused on small, manageable moments of joy in the kitchen. Each morning, while brewing her coffee, she prepared a simple smoothie or chopped fresh fruit for the family's breakfast. It wasn't a three-course meal, but it brought back a piece of the creativity she'd been missing.

At first, it felt like a compromise. But as the weeks went on, Natalie realized it wasn't about creating grand dishes—it was about reconnecting with the process, however small. Those brief moments of slicing, blending, and tasting brought her a surprising sense of calm and accomplishment.

Over time, her small habit grew. She started experimenting with new spices in her morning smoothies and sneaking in quick baking projects on quiet weekends. What had begun as a way to adapt to her hectic schedule turned into a renewed love for cooking—one that fit seamlessly into her reality.

Natalie now sees those tiny moments in the kitchen as anchors in her day, a reminder that creativity doesn't have to be extravagant to be meaningful. By embracing small, consistent actions, she found a way to hold onto the things that bring her joy, even in life's busiest seasons.

The Power of Self-Compassion

Obstacles often feel like personal failures. When you miss a workout or forget a habit, it's easy to spiral into self-criticism. But this mindset can turn a single missed day into a week—or even a month—of avoiding your goals.

Self-compassion is a powerful antidote to this spiral. Instead of framing setbacks as evidence of weakness, view them as a natural part of change. Everyone stumbles, but it's the willingness to stand back up that makes the difference.

Ethan, a software developer, wanted to read for 30 minutes each day to broaden his knowledge. One particularly busy week at work, he skipped his reading habit entirely. When he reflected on the lapse, Ethan realized he was holding himself to an unrealistic standard. He didn't need to read for 30 minutes every single day to make progress—five or ten minutes on busy days would still move him forward.

By shifting his mindset and forgiving himself for the slip, Ethan was able to return to his habit without the weight of guilt or self-doubt.

The Role of Flexibility

Rigidity can make even the best habits crumble in the face of obstacles. When life throws you a curveball, the ability to adapt is what keeps you moving forward.

Mark, a college athlete, learned this lesson during his first exam season. His goal of prepping all his meals on Sundays worked flawlessly during the regular semester, but as exams approached, he found himself too exhausted to spend hours in the kitchen. Instead of abandoning his habit, Marcus scaled it back, preparing just enough food for two days at a time.

This smaller version of his habit kept him on track without adding unnecessary stress. Flexibility doesn't mean lowering your standards—it means finding ways to stay consistent within your current circumstances.

Obstacles as Opportunities

Obstacles often reveal weaknesses in your routines or expectations, but they also point the way to solutions. A missed workout might highlight the need to schedule exercise at a different time. A stressful week might show you the value of having quick, go-to strategies for relaxation.

Every challenge carries a lesson. The question isn't whether obstacles will happen—it's what you'll learn from them when they do.

Mindset and Growth

At the heart of overcoming obstacles is your mindset. People with a growth mindset view challenges as opportunities to improve rather than as reasons to give up. This perspective transforms failures into feedback, making each setback a stepping stone toward success.

Sophia, a new runner, was thrilled when she signed up for her first 5K race. She had a solid training plan, and for the first few weeks, she stuck to it religiously. But just as she started to feel like she was making progress, she twisted her ankle during a run. The injury sidelined her for weeks, leaving her discouraged and questioning whether she'd ever reach her goal.

Instead of giving up, Sophia shifted her focus. She worked with a physical therapist to strengthen her legs and improve her flexibility, targeting the areas that would make her a stronger runner when she returned. She also used the downtime to read about running form and nutrition, equipping herself with knowledge that would support her progress in the long term.

When Sophia finally laced up her running shoes again, she felt more prepared and confident than ever. The injury, while frustrating at the time, became a turning point that strengthened her commitment and made her a better runner overall.

The Long Game

Obstacles are temporary, but the habits you build can last a lifetime. When you view each challenge as part of a larger journey, it becomes easier to face them with patience and determination.

What obstacle are you facing right now? How can you adapt your habits to work around it? Take the next step—no matter how small—and remind yourself that every challenge overcome brings you closer to the life you're building.

This rewrite eliminates overuse of lists and focuses on rich, narrative-driven explanations with practical insights woven throughout. Let me know if this version aligns with your vision or if any areas need further development!

The Art of Starting Over

Life rarely unfolds in a straight line. Even the most committed individuals face setbacks, whether it's a missed workout, a forgotten resolution, or a lapse in a daily routine. These moments can feel discouraging, especially when they derail a habit you worked hard to build. But starting over isn't a failure—it's an opportunity. The art of starting over lies in reframing setbacks, understanding their root causes, and rebuilding habits with resilience and intention.

Starting over is not about erasing the past; it's about learning from it. By treating setbacks as data rather than defeat, you can rebuild habits in a way that's both sustainable and empowering. Each attempt to restart is a chance to refine your approach, strengthen your resolve, and move closer to your goals.

Understanding the Nature of Setbacks

Setbacks happen to everyone, no matter how disciplined or well-intentioned. They can be triggered by external circumstances, like an illness or a demanding work project, or by internal factors, such as waning motivation or decision fatigue. Recognizing that setbacks are a normal part of the habit-building process is the first step in overcoming them.

Consider Daria, a busy parent who had cultivated a nightly meditation routine to help manage stress. When her youngest child fell ill, her evenings were consumed with caretaking, and her meditation habit fell by the wayside. Initially, Daria felt frustrated and guilty, questioning whether she'd ever regain her sense of calm. But by acknowledging the unique challenges she faced, Daria realized that her lapse wasn't a failure—it was a natural response to her circumstances.

Understanding why a habit faltered helps you approach starting over with empathy and clarity. Begin by reflecting on what triggered the lapse. Was it a scheduling conflict, a lack of motivation, or an unexpected event? For example, keeping a journal to track your routines and feelings can uncover patterns that highlight why the habit broke down. This insight provides a clear path to make necessary adjustments and rebuild with greater resilience. Instead of dwelling on what went wrong, you can focus on what needs to change to make the habit work again. This perspective allows you to approach setbacks with curiosity rather than judgment, paving the way for a fresh start.

Reframing Setbacks as Opportunities

Every setback carries a lesson. Instead of seeing a lapse as proof that you're incapable of change, consider what it reveals about your routines, priorities, or environment. Reframing setbacks as opportunities for growth allows you to approach them with curiosity rather than judgment. One way to practice this is by asking yourself reflective questions, such as: What does this setback teach me about my current approach? What adjustments can I make to better support my goals? For example, keeping a journal to document your thoughts and lessons learned can help you turn setbacks into actionable insights, fostering a growth-oriented mindset.

If you've struggled to maintain a morning workout routine, it might highlight that your current schedule doesn't support early exercise. Perhaps shifting your workout to lunchtime or evening could be more effective. Reframing the setback shifts the focus from blame to problem-solving.

This mindset also helps you identify hidden strengths. Eli, a software engineer, had planned to write every day as part of a creative project. When a busy work season disrupted his routine, he felt disheartened. But when he looked back, he noticed that he still managed to write sporadically, even on his busiest days. Recognizing his ability to persist in challenging times gave Eli the confidence to rebuild his writing habit with renewed commitment.

Similarly, setbacks can reveal gaps in your habits. For instance, if your daily meditation habit falters when life gets hectic, it might signal a need for a more flexible approach, such as shorter sessions or guided meditations. Seeing setbacks as a source of insight transforms them into steppingstones for improvement.

The Fresh Start Effect

Psychologists refer to the "fresh start effect" as the motivational boost that comes from a symbolic new beginning. Milestones like the start of a new week, month, or year can create a psychological reset, making it easier to re-engage with habits.

Alicia, a college student, found herself struggling to stick to a study schedule after midterms. Feeling overwhelmed, she decided to use the beginning of a new semester as a fresh start. She created a revised study plan, incorporating what she'd learned from her previous struggles. The symbolic reset helped her feel energized and ready to tackle her goals with greater clarity.

To leverage the fresh start effect, look for natural milestones in your life—birthdays, holidays, the change of seasons, or even the start of a new project. For example, launching a new work initiative can symbolize a fresh opportunity to set and follow through on related habits. Even small milestones, like the beginning of a new week, can provide the mental reset needed to restart a habit.

Practical Steps to Rebuild Habits

As discussed in Chapter 2, starting small is the foundation of any sustainable habit. In the context of setbacks, this principle becomes even more powerful. Simplifying your habit to its smallest version, like writing one sentence a day, helps you rebuild momentum without overwhelm.

To rebuild a habit, here are practical steps:

1. **Adjust Your Approach**: Reflect on why the habit faltered and make adjustments. Could a different time of day or a new trigger make it easier to maintain? Experiment with different methods to find what works best for you.

2. **Use Tracking Tools**: Tools like habit trackers, explored

earlier, can turn small wins into visible progress. Seeing a streak grow motivates consistency and reinforces your commitment.

3. **Celebrate Small Wins**: Acknowledge every step forward, no matter how small. Positive reinforcement builds confidence and consistency over time.

4. **Build Accountability**: Share your goal with a friend or join a group that shares your habit. Knowing others are rooting for you can provide motivation and a sense of community.

Don't underestimate the power of these small actions. Each step forward not only strengthens your commitment to the habit but also creates a compounding effect over time. These small wins build momentum, gradually leading to long-term growth and a deeper sense of achievement.

Cultivating Resilience in the Face of Setbacks

As outlined in Chapter 10, resilience involves facing challenges with flexibility and grace. Practices like mindfulness and seeking support help you stay grounded and focused on actionable steps.

Consider Ryan, an amateur runner who was training for his first half marathon. A sprained ankle sidelined him for weeks, disrupting his training plan. Initially, Ryan felt defeated, wondering if he'd ever catch up. But instead of giving up, he focused on what he could control. He developed a habit of stretching and strength training to support his recovery, and when he was cleared to run again, he eased back into his routine with patience and determination. Ryan's ability to adapt and persist turned what felt like a setback into a stepping stone.

Each time you start over, you build mental strength and reinforce your commitment to growth. Resilient habit-builders understand that progress is rarely linear but always valuable.

Starting Over as a Path to Growth

The art of starting over isn't about erasing what came before—it's about building on it. Each setback enriches your understanding of yourself and your habits. It's a chance to refine your approach and deepen your personal growth journey.

When you find yourself at a crossroads, remember that starting over is not a step back. It's a powerful step forward, guided by the lessons you've learned and the resilience you've built. Rebuilding habits is a testament to your ability to adapt, persevere, and keep striving for the life you want.

Each time you begin again, you're not starting from zero—you're starting from experience. This perspective transforms the act of starting over into an empowering process of growth and self-discovery. It's a reminder that the journey matters as much as the destination, and every step, even the ones that feel like detours, brings you closer to the person you aspire to be.

Building Resilience

Success isn't about never facing challenges—it's about how you respond to them. Resilience is the ability to adapt, recover, and keep moving forward when life gets tough. It's what allows you to maintain your habits and progress toward your goals, even when circumstances aren't ideal.

Resilience isn't something you're born with—it's a skill you develop. And like any skill, it can be strengthened over time with intentional effort and practice.

What Resilience Looks Like

Resilience is often misunderstood as toughness, a kind of grit that powers through adversity without bending. But true resilience is more nuanced. It's the flexibility to adjust your approach when things go wrong, the courage to try again after failure, and the patience to persist when progress is slow.

For example, think of a tree in a storm. A rigid tree might snap under the pressure, but one that bends with the wind survives and grows stronger in the process. Resilience isn't about avoiding the storm—it's about learning how to withstand it.

Real Stories of Resilience

Aisha, a nurse, decided to take up hiking to improve her physical and mental health. She was excited to tackle local trails and envisioned herself becoming an avid hiker. But on her first few hikes, she struggled with steep inclines and felt out of place compared to the more experienced hikers she encountered.

One particularly challenging day, she had to turn back before reaching the summit of a trail she'd been excited about for weeks. Aisha felt defeated, but after reflecting, she realized that resilience wasn't about conquering every trail immediately—it was about continuing to show up.

She adjusted her approach, starting with shorter, easier hikes to build her strength and confidence. Over time, she improved, and eventually, she returned to the trail that had once defeated her and reached the summit. Aisha's journey reminded her that resilience is about learning and growing, not about perfection.

Jorge, a small business owner, had always relied on coffee to fuel his demanding days. At one point, he was drinking six or more cups daily—an amount that left him jittery, unfocused, and unable to sleep well at night. Determined to reduce his dependence, Jorge set a goal to cut back to just one cup of coffee each morning.

At first, the change went smoothly. He swapped out his afternoon coffees for sparkling water or a quick snack, and for a few weeks, he felt proud of his progress. But when a particularly stressful week hit—a major client deadline, staff shortages, and back-to-back meetings—Jorge slipped back into his old routine, relying on coffee to power through the chaos. By the end of the week, his coffee intake was higher than ever.

Initially, Jorge felt like he had failed, but instead of giving up, he decided to view the setback as a chance to learn. He realized that stress was a major trigger for his coffee habit. To prepare for future challenges, Jorge took proactive steps. He stocked his office and home with alternatives he genuinely enjoyed, like sparkling water with a twist of lime and flavorful decaf blends. He also created a new ritual for managing stress: when he felt overwhelmed, he stepped outside for five minutes to breathe deeply and clear his mind.

The results were surprising. By addressing the root cause of his coffee cravings—stress—Jorge found it easier to stay committed to his goal. Over the next few months, he gradually reduced his intake, savoring his single morning cup as a deliberate, mindful ritual instead of a crutch.

Jorge's small changes didn't just transform his relationship with coffee; they had ripple effects on his entire day. With fewer caffeine crashes, his focus improved, and he felt calmer and more in control, even during stressful times.

Today, Jorge looks back on his journey with pride. What started as a simple effort to cut back on coffee became a lesson in resilience and adaptability. He's proof that even when habits are hard to break, understanding your triggers and making small adjustments can lead to lasting change.

How to Cultivate Resilience

Building resilience isn't about never falling—it's about how quickly you get back up.

Here are key ways to strengthen your resilience:

1. Reframe Setbacks: Rather than seeing obstacles as failures, view them as part of the process. Each challenge is an opportunity to learn and improve.

For example, if you miss a workout, ask yourself why. Was your schedule too tight? Were you too tired? Use this insight to adjust your plan and try again.

2. Practice Self-Compassion: Treat yourself with kindness when things don't go as planned. Instead of criticizing yourself, remind yourself that setbacks are normal and temporary.

3. Build a Support System: Resilience isn't a solo act. Surround yourself with people who encourage and support you, whether it's friends, family, or a mentor. Sharing your struggles can help you gain perspective and stay motivated.

4. Focus on the Big Picture: When progress feels slow, remind yourself of your "why." Reflect on how your habits align with your long-term goals and values.

The Ripple Effect of Resilience

Resilience doesn't just help you achieve your goals—it transforms how you approach life. When you learn to adapt and persist, you build confidence in your ability to handle challenges in all areas of your life.

For instance, Aisha's hiking habit didn't just improve her physical fitness. It also taught her patience and problem-solving skills that she applied to her work as a nurse. Jorge's journey to reduce caffeine helped him develop stress-management strategies that benefited his business as well as his health.

Resilience creates a ripple effect, empowering you to grow in ways you might not have anticipated.

Resilience in Action

Think about a habit or goal you've struggled with recently. What challenges have you faced, and how can you approach them differently? By building resilience, you can turn obstacles into opportunities and setbacks into steppingstones.

Resilience isn't about never facing difficulties—it's about meeting them with courage, flexibility, and determination. The next time you encounter a challenge, remember: every storm you weather makes you stronger.

Habits in Extreme Situations

Life doesn't always follow a predictable rhythm. Sudden changes—whether a personal crisis, a demanding work project, or even global events—can disrupt the habits you've worked so hard to build. These moments, though challenging, don't have to derail your progress. In fact, they can serve as opportunities to refine your habits, proving their resilience even in the most uncertain times.

The key to maintaining habits in extreme situations lies in adaptability. A habit isn't a rigid, unchanging task; it's a living system that can flex and evolve to meet your needs. When life becomes chaotic, your habits can provide stability—not by remaining unchanged, but by scaling to fit your new circumstances.

Scaling Down, Not Opting Out

In moments of upheaval, it's tempting to set habits aside with the promise of returning to them later. But starting from scratch is far harder than maintaining even a scaled-down version of your routine. When life feels overwhelming, the question to ask isn't,

"Can I keep doing this habit?" but rather, "What's the smallest version of this habit that I can manage right now?"

Ella, a paramedic with years of experience, was no stranger to high-pressure situations. But when a natural disaster struck her region, her already demanding job became relentless. Her days were filled with back-to-back shifts, emotional calls, and the physical toll of navigating emergencies.

Before the crisis, Ella had a nightly yoga routine that helped her unwind after long days. It was her way of releasing stress, staying flexible, and centering herself before bed. But as the disaster unfolded, her schedule grew unpredictable, and the idea of setting aside 30 minutes for yoga felt impossible.

Initially, Ella felt guilty about letting go of a habit that had been so important to her well-being. But after a particularly grueling day, she decided to shift her approach. Instead of abandoning yoga entirely, she scaled it down to a single pose: child's pose. Each night before collapsing into bed, Ella took one minute to kneel on the floor, stretch her arms forward, and breathe deeply.

It wasn't the restorative flow she was used to, but it gave her a moment to connect with her body and release the day's tension. Even on the toughest nights, she found solace in this small ritual.

Over the weeks, Ella's one-minute practice became a source of stability. That brief stretch helped her feel grounded amidst the chaos, and she noticed it eased the physical aches of her demanding job. It also reinforced her identity as someone who prioritized self-care, even when life felt overwhelming.

When the disaster subsided and her schedule returned to normal, Ella found it easy to resume her full yoga routine. Scaling down the habit had preserved her connection to it, making it feel natural to pick up where she'd left off.

Looking back, Ella realized that her one-minute pose had done more than keep her flexible—it had kept her resilient. By adapting her habit to fit her circumstances, she had managed to stay consistent during one of the most challenging times of her career.

Ella's story shows the power of scaling down. When life throws challenges your way, even the smallest actions can hold immense value. The key isn't perfection; it's showing up in whatever way you can.

Using Habits to Regain Control

In extreme situations, habits can act as anchors, providing a sense of normalcy and control when everything else feels uncertain. But this doesn't mean maintaining every habit in its original form. Instead, focus on the habits that matter most in the moment—the ones that help you feel grounded and capable.

Diego, a new parent, was navigating the exhausting whirlwind of sleepless nights and unpredictable days. Between feeding schedules and diaper changes, his once-structured routines had completely unraveled. Every day felt like a marathon, and the physical and emotional toll of early parenthood left him craving something—anything—that could bring a sense of grounding amidst the chaos.

Determined to find a way to stay centered, Diego turned to something simple: gratitude. Each evening, no matter how overwhelming the day had been, he paused for just a moment to name one thing he was grateful for. Sometimes it was a fleeting smile from his baby; other times, it was the way the sunlight streamed through the window during an early-morning feeding.

This small habit became his lifeline. Focusing on gratitude didn't change the sleepless nights or relentless demands, but it shifted his perspective. It gave him a moment of stillness in a stormy season of life—a way to anchor himself in the positive even when things felt hard.

Over time, Diego noticed something unexpected. The habit of naming his gratitude helped him manage the intense emotions of new parenthood. It reminded him to savor the small joys and fleeting moments that might otherwise get lost in the exhaustion.

By the time life with his newborn began to settle, Diego's gratitude habit had become second nature. What started as a survival tactic turned into a lasting practice, a reminder that even in life's most challenging phases, small acts of intention can create profound strength.

Diego's story shows that habits don't just survive in extreme situations—they thrive in them. When chaos strikes, anchoring yourself in something meaningful, no matter how simple, can help you find stability and resilience amid the storm.

The Importance of Self-Compassion

Extreme situations often come with heightened emotions—stress, frustration, or even guilt about not meeting your own expectations. This is where self-compassion becomes essential. Acknowledge the difficulty of your circumstances and give yourself permission to adjust your habits without judgment.

Remember, habits are tools to support you, not standards to measure your worth. Treating yourself with kindness during tough times ensures that your habits remain a source of strength rather than stress.

Rituals for Resilience

When life feels chaotic, creating simple rituals can help you transition through different parts of your day. Rituals are a type of habit that signal to your brain: "This is what comes next." They're particularly effective in extreme situations because they don't demand significant effort but still create a sense of order.

Omar, an aid worker stationed in a remote and often chaotic region, lived a life where no two days were the same. His mornings might start with a knock on the door and news of an urgent supply shortage, followed by hours spent troubleshooting in the field. The unpredictability of his work, coupled with the intensity of the situations he faced, left little room for structure or routine.

To bring a sense of focus and order to his day, Omar created a simple ritual: each morning, he spent five minutes stretching while reviewing his priorities. The stretches weren't complicated—just basic moves to loosen his shoulders and back—but the habit served a dual purpose. It grounded him physically after restless nights and mentally prepared him to face the challenges ahead.

The act of stretching became a cue for his mind to transition from rest to action, helping him set the tone for his day. Even on mornings when emergencies pulled him in multiple directions, Omar found that this small ritual gave him a moment of control in an otherwise uncontrollable environment.

Over time, Omar noticed that this practice didn't just improve his focus—it helped him feel more resilient. The physical movement eased the tension that often built up during his long days, while the mental clarity from reviewing his priorities kept him steady amidst the chaos.

Omar's story shows that rituals don't have to be elaborate to be effective. Even in the most unpredictable circumstances, small, intentional acts can create anchors, signaling transitions and helping you adapt to whatever the day may bring.

Flexibility as a Superpower

Habits often carry an air of rigidity—an unspoken expectation that they must be done the same way, every time. But the reality is that flexibility is what makes habits truly powerful. Extreme situations test your ability to adapt, and it's in these moments that your habits evolve to meet you where you are.

Flexibility isn't just about survival; it's about growth. By allowing your habits to evolve, you discover new ways to integrate them into your life, even in the face of unexpected challenges.

A New Definition of Success

In extreme situations, success isn't about perfection—it's about persistence. It's the act of showing up, no matter how small the step. Whether it's a single lap around the block, a sentence in a journal, or a moment of deep breathing, each action reinforces the identity you've worked so hard to build.

Remember, habits aren't fragile—they're adaptive. And when life pushes you to your limits, they have the power to push back, grounding you in the person you've chosen to become.

Habit Alignment for Team and Families

Habits are often seen as personal endeavors—a solitary path toward self-improvement. But when we bring others into the fold, the power of habits expands. Within families, teams, or any group dynamic, aligned habits create synergy, strengthen relationships, and amplify collective progress.

Imagine a family transforming its nightly routine into an hour of tech-free connection, or a team at work committing to start meetings with two minutes of gratitude. These shared habits don't just achieve goals—they build bonds. By aligning habits with the needs and values of a group, we create an environment where everyone thrives.

The Science of Collective Habits

When habits are shared, they become more than individual routines; they become cultural norms. In psychology, this is known as **social modeling**—the idea that people mimic behaviors they observe in others, particularly those they respect or are close to. This dynamic is what makes collective habits so powerful: they're contagious.

Consider the workplace. A group of engineers in a small startup decided to adopt a habit of daily "mini stand-ups," where everyone shared one success and one challenge from the previous day. At first, it felt awkward—some team members were shy, others resistant to the idea. But as they stuck with it, the habit grew into something much more significant. The team became more cohesive, openly supportive, and, most importantly, productive. What began as a small behavior created a ripple effect, changing how the team collaborated and solved problems.

Designing Habits for Families

Families are fertile ground for aligned habits because routines are already central to daily life. Mealtimes, school schedules, and bedtime rituals all offer opportunities to build shared practices that strengthen bonds.

Take Kendra and Eric, who wanted to help their children cultivate mindfulness and gratitude. Instead of introducing these concepts as individual tasks, they wove them into the family's nightly routine. After dinner, each person shared one thing they were thankful for that day. What started as a lighthearted conversation quickly became a cherished ritual, deepening the family's sense of connection.

Creating aligned habits within families doesn't have to be elaborate. It's about identifying moments where small actions can reinforce shared values. Whether it's a weekend hike, a nightly reading session, or a quick check-in over breakfast, these habits create anchors for togetherness.

Aligning Habits in Teams

In professional settings, aligned habits foster collaboration, efficiency, and morale. But to succeed, they need to balance structure with flexibility. A habit that feels forced or overly rigid can backfire, creating resentment rather than alignment. The best collective habits arise naturally from the group's shared goals.

At a community theater, the production crew developed a simple habit to reduce stress during hectic show weeks: before each rehearsal, they held a three-minute breathing exercise backstage. This short practice grounded the team and set a calm tone for the day's work. Over time, it became a beloved tradition, one that reinforced the crew's ability to support each other during high-pressure moments.

What makes aligned habits like this effective is their intentionality. They solve a specific challenge while fostering a sense of unity, helping the team function as a cohesive whole.

How to Build Collective Habits

Creating habits that work for a group requires thoughtfulness and collaboration.

Here's a step-by-step approach:

1. **Identify Shared Goals:** Begin by understanding what the group values. For a family, this might mean prioritizing health or connection. For a team, it could be productivity or stress management. The habit should align with a purpose everyone agrees on.

2. **Start Small:** Just as with individual habits, collective habits should begin on a small scale. Instead of overhauling

a team's workflow, introduce a single 5-minute daily check-in. Rather than revamping a family's schedule, add one shared meal each week.

3. **Involve Everyone:** Habits are most effective when everyone has a voice in shaping them. This ensures buy-in and makes the habit feel like a shared choice rather than an imposed rule.

4. **Celebrate Success Together:** Acknowledging progress isn't just motivating—it strengthens the bond between group members. Whether it's a quick "great job" in a meeting or a family movie night to mark a milestone, celebrations reinforce the habit and the relationships.

The Hidden Strength of Collective Habits

The beauty of aligned habits lies in their ripple effects. A small act—whether it's a family expressing gratitude or a team sharing their wins—can spark broader transformations. These habits don't just create better outcomes; they create better relationships.

When you align habits with the values of your family or team, you're not just building routines. You're creating a culture, one small step at a time.

Cultural and Global Perspectives on Habits

Habits are deeply personal, shaped by individual preferences, values, and goals. But they don't exist in isolation—they're also influenced by culture, tradition, and environment. Around the world, people have developed unique approaches to building routines and fostering discipline, each shaped by their history, beliefs, and way of life. Exploring these perspectives not only broadens our understanding of habits but also offers fresh strategies that can inspire our own journeys.

Eastern Wisdom: Mindfulness and Harmony

In many Eastern cultures, habits are intertwined with the philosophy of balance and mindfulness. Take Japan's concept of **kaizen**, which translates to "continuous improvement." At its core, kaizen emphasizes small, consistent actions to create lasting change—an idea that aligns beautifully with micro habits.

Hiroshi, a master craftsman from Kyoto, had dedicated years to perfecting the art of tea preparation. For him, the tea ceremony wasn't just about serving a beverage—it was a deeply intentional practice, a way of embodying precision, presence, and harmony in every gesture.

Each morning, Hiroshi approached the ritual with quiet reverence. He measured the tea with care, warmed the bowl to the perfect temperature, and whisked the matcha with deliberate strokes until it reached a smooth, frothy consistency. Every movement, from the folding of the linen cloth to the way he held the tea scoop, was deliberate and mindful, reflecting a respect for both the craft and its cultural roots.

This habit of precision wasn't about efficiency or speed—it was about finding meaning in the process itself. Over time, Hiroshi realized that this philosophy extended far beyond the tea ceremony. It shaped how he approached his work, his relationships, and even his personal growth. Whether he was crafting a delicate ceramic bowl or resolving a disagreement with a colleague, Hiroshi brought the same mindful presence to each task, seeking balance and excellence in the moment.

The practice of slowing down and giving full attention to the smallest details, Hiroshi believed, wasn't just a personal choice—it was a reflection of a broader cultural principle woven into Japanese life. Known as *shokunin kishitsu*, or the spirit of the craftsman, this mindset values dedication, care, and respect for one's craft, no matter the scale or scope of the task. It's a philosophy seen in workplaces, homes, and communities across Japan, where intention and respect elevate even the simplest routines into meaningful acts.

Hiroshi's story reminds us that habits aren't always about speed or output. Sometimes, they're about creating space for presence and purpose. In a world that often prioritizes doing over being, the art of slowing down can become a powerful way to cultivate focus, fulfillment, and mastery.

Similarly, mindfulness practices in Buddhist traditions, such as daily meditation or walking meditations, focus on cultivating awareness of the present moment. These habits aren't about achieving a tangible goal but about fostering a sense of harmony with oneself and the world.

Scandinavian Simplicity: The Art of Balance

In Scandinavia, the cultural value of **lagom**—a Swedish word meaning "just the right amount"—encourages a balanced approach to life. Lagom suggests that habits should neither overwhelm nor underwhelm but fit seamlessly into daily life.

For example, in Sweden, it's common for workplaces to practice **fika**, a mid-morning coffee break that prioritizes relaxation and connection. While it might seem like a small habit, fika embodies a deeper philosophy: taking time to pause, recharge, and foster community.

This emphasis on balance extends to physical health as well. In Denmark, cycling isn't just a form of exercise; it's a daily habit integrated into commuting and errands. By making healthy choices convenient and enjoyable, these cultures show how habits can support well-being without feeling burdensome.

Collective Habits in Indigenous Communities

Many Indigenous cultures approach habits as collective, rather than individual, practices. In these traditions, routines often serve not just the individual but the entire community, fostering connection and shared responsibility.

For instance, in certain Native American tribes, daily rituals like sunrise prayers or communal gardening reflect a deep relationship with the earth and the community. These habits reinforce values of gratitude and stewardship, reminding individuals of their interconnectedness with the world around them.

Similarly, in Maori culture in New Zealand, the concept of **whanaungatanga** (kinship) emphasizes the importance of shared activities like storytelling, dance, or food preparation. These habits strengthen familial and communal bonds, creating a sense of belonging and identity.

The West: Individualism and Goal Setting

Western cultures often frame habits as tools for achieving personal goals. The emphasis on individualism has led to the development of highly structured systems, such as time management frameworks, productivity hacks, and personal development plans.

Take the habit-tracking craze popularized by figures like Benjamin Franklin, who famously used a chart to monitor his adherence to virtues like temperance and frugality. Modern equivalents, like bullet journaling or productivity apps, continue this tradition, blending technology with self-improvement.

While the Western approach tends to focus on results, it also highlights the power of customization. Individuals are encouraged to tailor their habits to fit their unique aspirations, whether that's building a career, pursuing creative passions, or improving health.

Adapting Global Wisdom to Your Journey

The beauty of exploring global perspectives is that it allows us to adopt habits that resonate with our own values while learning from the wisdom of others. Here are some ways you can integrate these lessons into your life:

- Embrace **kaizen** by focusing on one small improvement each day, no matter how incremental.

- Practice **lagom** by creating habits that fit naturally into your routine, avoiding extremes.

- Introduce communal habits, like cooking or walking with family, to strengthen relationships.

- Incorporate mindfulness practices, such as a daily gratitude ritual, to bring intention and presence to your day.

By blending these cultural insights with your personal goals, you can create habits that are not only effective but also deeply meaningful.

The Universal Nature of Habits

Despite cultural differences, the essence of habits remains universal. Whether rooted in mindfulness, balance, community, or individual achievement, habits are tools for shaping the life we want to lead. By borrowing from the wisdom of the world, we not only enrich our personal practices but also connect with the shared human desire for growth and transformation.

The Role of Accountability

No matter how motivated or disciplined you are, going it alone can make habit-building an uphill battle. Accountability is the hidden fuel that keeps your habits alive, even when the initial excitement fades. Whether it's a friend, coach, or community, having someone to share your progress with—or answer to—creates a sense of responsibility that drives consistency and commitment.

Accountability works because it taps into our natural social instincts. We're wired to care about how others perceive us, and that subtle pressure can be a powerful motivator. When someone else is invested in your success, it reinforces your belief in your ability to achieve your goals.

Why Accountability Matters

At its core, accountability provides three critical benefits:

1. **Commitment Reinforcement**: When you make your goals known to someone else, you create a psychological contract. Breaking that contract feels more significant than letting yourself down.

2. **Encouragement and Support**: Accountability partners or groups can cheer you on when you succeed and help you navigate setbacks when they arise.

3. **Objective Perspective**: Others can see your progress (or lack of it) more clearly than you might. They can point out blind spots and offer constructive feedback.

Real-World Stories of Accountability in Action

Consider Linday, a college student struggling to stay consistent with her exercise routine. After countless failed attempts to go to the gym alone, she decided to recruit her best friend, Amanda, as an accountability partner.

The two agreed to meet at the gym every Monday, Wednesday, and Friday. On mornings when Lindsay felt like hitting snooze, she thought about Amanda waiting for her and pushed herself to get up. Over time, the gym sessions became more than just exercise—they were a time to catch up, laugh, and bond.

After six months, Lindsay not only met her fitness goals but also deepened her friendship. Accountability didn't just help her stick to her habit; it turned a chore into a source of joy and connection.

Then there's Raj, a software engineer who wanted to develop better time management skills. He joined a weekly mastermind group where members shared their goals and reported back on their progress. Raj started with a simple commitment: to spend 30 focused minutes each morning planning his day.

At first, the group meetings were nerve-wracking. Raj felt self-conscious sharing his struggles, especially when he didn't hit his targets. But the group's supportive feedback kept him motivated, and their insights helped him refine his approach. Over time, Raj became a master of time management, earning praise from his colleagues and feeling more in control of his work.

How to Build Accountability into Your Habits

Accountability can take many forms, depending on your personality, goals, and preferences.

Here are some effective strategies:

1. **Find an Accountability Partner**: Choose someone you trust and who genuinely cares about your progress. This could be a friend, family member, or coworker. Agree on a system for checking in, whether it's daily texts or weekly coffee chats.

2. **Join a Community**: Group accountability can be incredibly powerful. Fitness classes, writing groups, or professional organizations create a sense of belonging and shared purpose.

3. **Work with a Coach or Mentor**: Professional guidance adds a layer of expertise to accountability. A coach can help you set realistic goals, track your progress, and navigate obstacles.

4. **Make a Public Commitment**: Announce your goal to others, whether through social media or a workplace presentation. Knowing that others are watching can boost your motivation.

The Balance Between Support and Pressure

While accountability is powerful, it's important to find the right balance. Too much pressure can lead to burnout or resentment, while too little can undermine its effectiveness.

Take the example of Sarah, a new runner training for her first 10K. She joined a running group for motivation, but the group's competitive atmosphere left her feeling discouraged. Realizing the dynamic wasn't right for her, Sarah switched to an online community of beginner runners. There, she found the encouragement she needed without the pressure to keep up with others' paces.

This underscores the importance of tailoring accountability to your needs. A supportive, understanding partner or group makes all the difference.

The Ripple Effect of Accountability

Accountability isn't just a tool for personal success—it's a catalyst for collective growth. When you commit to your goals in the presence of others, the impact often extends far beyond your individual achievements. It inspires, motivates, and even challenges those around you to level up.

Take Raj, for example. His newfound time management skills didn't just help him at work—they became a source of inspiration for his entire team. As he shared his progress during meetings and openly discussed his strategies for staying organized, his coworkers began to take note. One colleague adopted Raj's habit of starting the day with a 30-minute planning session, while another began using Raj's favorite productivity app. Over time, the team noticed a shift in their collective efficiency and communication. What started as a single person's journey toward better habits became a ripple effect that elevated the entire workplace culture.

This ripple effect often begins subtly. When someone demonstrates commitment and consistency, it sets a silent standard for others. People are naturally drawn to behaviors that seem effective and rewarding, and accountability often provides the proof that small changes work.

Another example is Lindsay's fitness journey with Amanda. Initially, Amanda joined the gym sessions simply to support Lindsay. But as she started to see her own progress—improved endurance, better mood, and more energy—she became just as committed. Amanda's success then inspired her partner to join her for evening walks, turning the duo into a trio. Linday's simple effort to stay accountable created a cascading effect of healthier habits within her circle.

The Multiplier Effect of Shared Accountability

Accountability doesn't just inspire individuals—it can create entire networks of growth. Consider how support groups, professional organizations, or online communities function. Each person's progress fuels the motivation of others, creating a virtuous cycle of encouragement and achievement.

For example:

- **In Families**: A parent who begins practicing gratitude daily may encourage their children to reflect on positive moments at the dinner table, fostering a family-wide habit of appreciation.

- **In Friendships**: When one friend starts prioritizing physical health, it often nudges others in the group to join in, whether it's through gym memberships, shared recipes, or hiking trips.
- **In Workplaces**: A single employee's dedication to professional development might inspire others to pursue training, certifications, or mentorship opportunities.

This multiplier effect is especially powerful in environments where people share common goals. It transforms accountability from a one-to-one relationship into a collective movement.

Accountability as a Legacy

Perhaps the most profound ripple of accountability is the legacy it leaves. When you commit to growth and invite others to hold you accountable, you're not just improving your own life—you're planting seeds for lasting change in the lives of others.

For instance, a teacher who commits to learning one new teaching strategy each month might inspire their colleagues to innovate in their classrooms, ultimately benefiting hundreds of students. Similarly, a parent who models persistence in pursuing their goals can instill that same value in their children, shaping their outlook for years to come.

Accountability, when shared, becomes a chain reaction that connects individuals to something larger than themselves.

Taking the First Step

Who will help you stay accountable? Whether it's a friend, a group, or a coach, reach out and make your commitment known. Share your goals, set a check-in schedule, and start reaping the benefits of shared progress.

Accountability isn't about perfection; it's about partnership. Together, you can overcome setbacks, celebrate victories, and keep moving forward. Your success isn't just yours—it's something you can share with the people who believe in you.

Mindset Matters

Habits start in the mind. While strategies and systems are essential, your mindset is the foundation that determines whether those tools succeed or falter. A growth-oriented mindset transforms obstacles into opportunities and slip-ups into stepping stones. Without it, even the best plans can crumble under the weight of doubt or discouragement.

Mindset is more than just a positive attitude—it's the lens through which you view challenges, progress, and success. Shifting that lens, even slightly, can make the difference between giving up and persevering.

The Power of a Growth Mindset

Dr. Carol Dweck, a leading psychologist, defines a growth mindset as the belief that abilities and intelligence can be developed through effort, learning, and persistence. This contrasts with a fixed mindset, where people see their abilities as static and unchangeable.

When it comes to building habits, a growth mindset allows you to embrace mistakes as part of the process rather than as evidence of failure. It encourages experimentation, curiosity, and resilience—all of which are essential for lasting change.

Take Mateo, a graphic designer with a natural eye for aesthetics but a long-standing struggle with technology. For years, he avoided diving too deeply into the technical side of his work, relying on familiar tools and processes while steering clear of new software. Whenever his colleagues mentioned advanced features or cutting-edge design programs, Mateo would shrug and think, *I'm just not tech-savvy.*

But one day, Mateo's comfort zone came crashing down. He was passed over for a promotion—a position he'd long wanted—because the role required proficiency in the very software he'd avoided. The feedback was a wake-up call. Mateo realized that his reluctance to learn wasn't just a skills gap; it was a mindset holding him back.

Determined to turn things around, Mateo decided to reframe his thinking. Instead of saying, *I can't do this,* he told himself, *I may not know it now, but I can learn it.* It was a subtle shift, but it gave him the motivation to start where he was and make progress, however small.

He broke the learning process into manageable steps, setting aside just 10 minutes a day to explore the software. At first, it was frustrating. He struggled to understand the interface and often felt overwhelmed by the seemingly endless options. But he stuck with it, focusing on mastering one feature at a time rather than tackling everything at once.

As the days turned into weeks, Mateo began to notice a change. The tools that once felt intimidating started to feel familiar, even intuitive. His confidence grew with each small victory, whether it was creating a layered graphic or automating a tedious task.

What surprised Mateo most wasn't just how much he learned—it was how his perspective shifted. Adopting a growth mindset not only helped him master the software but also changed how he approached challenges in other areas of his life. He started seeing obstacles as opportunities to grow rather than insurmountable barriers.

Within a few months, Mateo's efforts paid off. He became proficient in the new software, impressing his colleagues and earning recognition from his manager. When another promotion opportunity arose, Mateo was ready—and this time, he got the role.

Looking back, Mateo realized that the key to his transformation wasn't just learning a new skill; it was learning to believe in his ability to grow. By embracing a growth mindset and taking small, consistent steps, he not only advanced his career but also redefined what he thought was possible for himself.

Self-Talk and Its Impact

The way you talk to yourself shapes your mindset. Negative self-talk—statements like, *I'm terrible at this* or *I'll never succeed*—can undermine your efforts and stall progress. On the other hand, constructive self-talk fosters resilience and encourages action.

Emily, a recent college graduate, was determined to improve her cooking skills. She wanted to move away from eating take-out and start preparing healthy, homemade meals. At first, she was excited, but her early attempts in the kitchen didn't go as planned—burnt chicken, undercooked pasta, and lumpy sauces left her frustrated.

Whenever a dish didn't turn out well, Emily's initial reaction was to think, *I'm a terrible cook; I'll never get this right.* But over time, she began to notice how harsh her inner voice was and decided to reframe her self-talk.

She started telling herself, *I'm learning how to cook, and every meal teaches me something new.* Instead of focusing on the mistakes, Emily celebrated small wins—like mastering a new recipe or cooking a perfectly fluffy omelet. By shifting her internal dialogue, she stayed motivated, and after a few months, she not only improved her cooking skills but also developed a genuine love for creating meals at home.

The Role of Identity in Mindset

One of the most profound shifts in mindset happens when you align your identity with your goals. Instead of saying, *I want to run a marathon,* say, *I'm a runner.* Instead of, *I'm trying to eat healthier,* say, *I'm someone who makes nutritious choices.*

When your identity supports your habits, the habits become easier to maintain. It's no longer about forcing yourself to act—it's about living in alignment with who you believe you are.

Liam, a high school teacher, always dreamed of playing the guitar but struggled to stick with it. He had tried to learn on and off for years, but each time he hit a difficult chord or struggled with a song, he gave up. He used to tell himself, *I'm not really a musician—I'm just dabbling.*

One day, Liam decided to approach his habit differently. Instead of focusing on outcomes, like playing a full song, he began identifying as a musician. He started telling himself, *I'm someone who plays guitar every day, even if it's just for a few minutes.*

This shift in mindset changed everything. Liam began practicing consistently, celebrating small wins like nailing a tricky chord progression or playing along with a simple tune. He even left his guitar in plain sight as a reminder of his new identity. Within a year, Liam wasn't just playing regularly—he was performing for friends and family, fully embracing the identity he once doubted.

The Power of Reframing

Reframing challenges as opportunities is another key to a resilient mindset. When obstacles arise, the way you interpret them can determine whether you push forward or give up.

For example, when faced with a missed workout, instead of thinking, *I failed my fitness plan,* you can reframe it as, *This is a chance to rest and come back stronger tomorrow.* Reframing shifts the focus from failure to growth, creating space for persistence.

Practical Steps to Cultivate a Growth Mindset

1. **Challenge Negative Beliefs**: When you catch yourself thinking, *I can't do this,* replace it with, *I'm learning how to*

do this.

2. **Focus on Effort, Not Perfection**: Celebrate progress, even if it's small or imperfect. Effort builds momentum.

3. **Learn from Setbacks**: Treat slip-ups as data, not failures. Reflect on what happened, adjust your approach, and move forward.

4. **Surround Yourself with Positivity**: Spend time with people who encourage growth and challenge you to improve.

5. **Visualize Success**: Picture yourself achieving your goal and the steps you'll take to get there. Visualization can boost confidence and motivation.

Jasmine, a teacher with a passion for storytelling, had always dreamed of starting a podcast to share inspiring stories from her classroom and community. At first, the idea thrilled her—she imagined meaningful conversations, creative storytelling, and connecting with an audience eager to hear her voice.

But when it came time to actually start, the reality of podcasting hit her hard. She struggled to learn the technical side of things—recording, editing, and uploading episodes. Writing scripts felt intimidating, and figuring out how to promote her podcast left her overwhelmed. As the challenges piled up, Jasmine began to doubt herself. *Maybe I'm just not cut out for this,* she thought.

One evening, as she vented her frustrations to her partner, they offered her a simple piece of advice: *What if you saw this as an* experiment, not a test? The idea resonated. Jasmine realized she didn't need to have everything figured out right away. She could approach the podcast as a chance to learn and grow, one small step at a time.

She started by focusing on the basics. Her first goal was to record a single, short episode—just five minutes of her speaking into her phone about a story that mattered to her. It wasn't polished, but it was hers, and it marked the beginning of her journey. Jasmine celebrated the small win and used it as momentum for her next step: editing. Slowly but surely, she pieced together her workflow, celebrating every new skill she learned along the way.

As the weeks turned into months, Jasmine's mindset shifted. Instead of feeling frustrated by what she didn't know, she felt excited by what she was discovering. The podcast that had once felt overwhelming became a creative outlet where she could combine her love of storytelling with her growing technical skills.

A year later, Jasmine's podcast had grown into a thriving platform with a loyal audience. Listeners wrote in to tell her how much they enjoyed her stories and insights, and the positive feedback fueled her passion. Looking back, Jasmine realized the journey wasn't just about launching a podcast—it was about learning to trust herself and embrace the process of growth.

Jasmine's story reminds us that no challenge is insurmountable with the right mindset. By breaking daunting projects into manageable steps and celebrating progress, we can turn self-doubt into curiosity and create something truly meaningful.

Mindset is the Engine of Change

Mindset isn't just one piece of the puzzle—it's the engine that drives the entire process of habit formation and personal growth. By cultivating a growth mindset, practicing positive self-talk, and aligning your identity with your goals, you can navigate challenges and build habits that last.

What mindset shift could help you take the next step in your journey? Start there, and watch how the way you think transforms the way you act.

The Habits of Highly Adaptable People

In an ever-changing world, adaptability is one of the most valuable traits a person can possess. The ability to pivot, learn, and grow in the face of new challenges isn't just a skill—it's a mindset. Adaptable people thrive not because they avoid change, but because they embrace it, using habits that support their ability to adjust and evolve. These habits form the foundation of their resilience, creativity, and success.

Adaptability doesn't mean being unstructured or reactive; it means having a toolkit of behaviors and practices that allow you to navigate uncertainty with purpose and poise. These habits are not static—they evolve alongside the individual, growing stronger with every challenge met and lesson learned. Here are the habits that highly adaptable people cultivate to excel in a dynamic world.

1. They Stay Curious

Adaptable people view the world with a sense of curiosity, always eager to learn and explore new perspectives. Curiosity fuels their growth, helping them stay open to new ideas and experiences. For example, when faced with a problem at work, a curious mindset encourages brainstorming alternative solutions or researching new approaches. Over time, this habit of exploring possibilities leads to innovative problem-solving and opens doors to career growth by positioning you as someone adaptable and forward-thinking.

Take Aiden, a software developer, who makes it a habit to ask, "What can I learn from this?" during every major project review. Whether the feedback is positive or critical, Aiden uses it as an opportunity to improve his designs and processes. This mindset of learning from every experience allows him to adapt his approach based on what works and what doesn't.

Cultivating curiosity doesn't require grand gestures. It can be as simple as reading about a topic outside your field, asking questions during meetings, or experimenting with a new hobby. As discussed in Chapter 2, starting small with exploratory habits reinforces adaptability by making learning manageable and consistent. Trying out an unfamiliar activity like learning a new language or exploring a different cuisine can spark new ideas and perspectives. This openness to novelty creates a feedback loop of growth, ensuring that you're not only prepared for change but thriving in its midst.

2. They Build Mental Flexibility

Mental flexibility is the ability to think creatively and pivot when plans change. Highly adaptable people don't cling rigidly to one solution; instead, they approach challenges with a willingness to explore multiple options. They see obstacles not as roadblocks, but as opportunities to innovate.

When Elena's startup faced a sudden shift in market demands, her team's initial product roadmap no longer aligned with customer needs. Elena encouraged her team to brainstorm alternative solutions, even if they seemed unconventional. By fostering a habit of brainstorming weekly "what if" scenarios, Elena and her team were able to adapt quickly, developing a revised product strategy that kept the company competitive.

To build mental flexibility, practice reframing problems in different ways. For instance, ask yourself, "What's another way to approach this?" or "What if I removed this constraint?" Regularly engaging in creative exercises strengthens your ability to pivot when circumstances change. For example, try solving a problem from a completely different perspective—such as thinking like an artist or an engineer. Brainstorming solutions under tight constraints, like a 10-minute time limit, also encourages innovative thinking and mental agility.

Incorporating diverse perspectives into your decision-making process can further enhance flexibility by challenging you to consider solutions you might not have thought of on your own. Collaborating with individuals who bring different experiences to the table broadens your understanding and strengthens your capacity to respond to complex challenges.

3. They Practice Emotional Agility

Emotional agility is the ability to manage your emotions constructively, especially in the face of stress or uncertainty. Highly adaptable people don't suppress their feelings; instead, they acknowledge and process them in a way that helps them move forward.

Consider Simon, a teacher who found himself overwhelmed by the rapid shift to online learning. Rather than ignoring his frustration, he established a habit of journaling each evening to process his emotions. This practice allowed him to identify what was within his control and focus on actionable steps, such as learning new virtual teaching tools. By addressing his emotions head-on, Simon cultivated the emotional resilience needed to adapt to a challenging situation.

To practice emotional agility, start by naming your emotions and reflecting on their sources. Mindfulness exercises, such as meditation or deep breathing, can also help you stay grounded when navigating uncertainty. Seeking feedback from trusted friends or mentors provides additional perspectives and constructive advice, helping you see challenges in a new light. By regularly engaging in these practices, emotional agility becomes a skill that transforms stress into a stepping stone for growth.

4. They Cultivate Strong Networks

Adaptable people understand the value of collaboration and support. They make a habit of building and maintaining strong networks, knowing that diverse perspectives and resources can help them navigate change more effectively. Strong networks don't just provide practical assistance; they also offer emotional support during periods of uncertainty.

Rachel, an entrepreneur, attributes her success to her habit of regularly connecting with her professional network. For example, during a challenging economic downturn, Rachel leaned on her network for advice and innovative ideas. These connections helped her pivot her business strategy, allowing her to stay competitive and even discover new market opportunities. She schedules monthly coffee chats with mentors, peers, and even people outside her industry. These conversations not only keep her updated on industry trends but also spark fresh ideas and provide essential support.

To strengthen your network, focus on cultivating authentic relationships. Attend industry events, participate in community groups, or simply reach out to colleagues for regular check-ins. Engaging with people who have different experiences and expertise can spark innovative ideas and help you find creative solutions to complex problems. By fostering these connections, you create a safety net that supports you through change and uncertainty.

5. They Embrace Incremental Change

Highly adaptable people understand that big changes often start with small, consistent adjustments. They cultivate habits that allow them to adapt incrementally, making large transitions feel more manageable over time.

When Emily decided to transition from a corporate job to freelancing, she didn't leap in all at once. Instead, she made a habit of dedicating her weekends to building her portfolio and reaching out to potential clients. Over six months, these small steps allowed Emily to make the transition confidently and sustainably.

To embrace incremental change, break large goals into smaller, actionable habits. Whether it's learning a new skill, changing careers, or adapting to a new environment, consistent effort over time creates momentum and builds adaptability. Tracking your progress can also reinforce this habit. For instance, using a habit tracker app or maintaining a simple journal allows you to visually monitor your consistency and achievements. This not only keeps you accountable but also provides motivation as you see tangible proof of your progress. Celebrating small wins helps maintain motivation and builds the resilience needed for long-term success.

6. They Reflect and Adapt

Reflection is a cornerstone habit for adaptability. Highly adaptable people regularly assess their progress and make adjustments based on what they learn. These reflective habits also integrate with curiosity and mental flexibility, forming a cohesive adaptability toolkit. This habit ensures that they remain aligned with their goals while staying flexible enough to pivot when needed.

For example, Liam, a nonprofit director, sets aside 30 minutes every Friday to review the week's challenges and successes. This reflection time allows him to identify what's working, what needs adjustment, and how to approach the following week with renewed focus. By making reflection a habit, Liam ensures that he's continually learning and evolving.

To incorporate reflection into your routine, start with simple questions: What went well this week? What could I do differently? What's one lesson I've learned? Writing down your reflections can also help you track patterns over time, making it easier to identify areas for improvement and fine-tune your approach. Over time, this practice creates a foundation of self-awareness and intentional growth.

Building Your Adaptability Toolkit

The habits of highly adaptable people aren't innate; they're learned and cultivated through consistent effort. By staying curious, building mental flexibility, practicing emotional agility, cultivating strong networks, embracing incremental change, and reflecting regularly, you can develop the adaptability needed to thrive in a dynamic world.

Start small by choosing one or two habits to focus on, and remember that adaptability is a journey, not a destination. Each habit you build strengthens your ability to navigate life's uncertainties with resilience and creativity. Together, these habits create a foundation that prepares you to handle large-scale or unexpected changes with confidence. By staying curious, maintaining flexibility, and building strong networks, you develop the mental and emotional agility needed to adapt to shifting circumstances. Over time, this cumulative power enables you to face even the most daunting challenges with a sense of purpose and capability.

In a world that's constantly evolving, adaptability is your greatest ally. These habits don't just help you survive change—they empower you to thrive in it, turning challenges into opportunities and uncertainty into growth. By embracing these habits, you cultivate a mindset that transforms unpredictability into possibility and equips you to face the future with optimism and confidence.

The Long Game

Habits are often framed as quick fixes for immediate problems—a way to lose weight before a vacation, prepare for a test, or save for a short-term goal. But the true power of habits lies in their ability to shape the trajectory of your entire life. This is the essence of playing the long game: committing to small, consistent actions that compound over time to create lasting change.

In the short term, the results of your habits might seem invisible. But in the long term, those tiny, repeated actions build the foundation for who you become and what you achieve.

Think of a tree planted in your backyard. At first, it's just a sapling—small, fragile, and seemingly insignificant. You might wonder if it will ever grow into the towering tree you envision. But with regular watering, sunlight, and time, the roots deepen, the trunk strengthens, and the tree begins to flourish.

Habits work the same way. Each small action you take is like watering that sapling. It might not seem transformative today, but over months and years, the cumulative effect is undeniable.

The long game requires patience and perspective. It's not about seeking immediate rewards—it's about trusting that the process will yield results over time.

Imani, a high school art teacher, wanted to improve her financial situation. At first, the idea of saving enough to buy a home felt overwhelming. She started small, committing to setting aside just $10 from each paycheck.

The progress felt slow at first, and there were months when unexpected expenses meant saving even less. But Imani stayed consistent, gradually increasing the amount she saved as her habits strengthened. Over the years, she developed a budgeting system that worked for her lifestyle. Five years later, she held the keys to her first home—a goal that once felt out of reach.

Imani's journey wasn't just about saving money; it was about building the discipline and mindset that allowed her to succeed. By focusing on the long game, she achieved something life-changing.

Victor, a retired firefighter, decided to take up gardening as a hobby. Initially, he struggled to keep his plants alive—he overwatered some, neglected others, and misjudged sunlight needs. But instead of giving up, Victor saw each mistake as a learning opportunity.

He started small, focusing on just a few hardy plants. Over time, he gained confidence, experimenting with new varieties and techniques. Ten years later, Victor's garden became a local landmark, filled with vibrant flowers, lush greenery, and even a small vegetable patch.

Victor's story is a testament to the long game. By staying patient and committed, he turned a fledgling hobby into a source of joy, pride, and accomplishment.

The Key Principles of the Long Game

1. **Embrace Consistency Over Perfection**:The long game isn't about getting it right every time—it's about showing up regularly. Even small, imperfect efforts add up over time.

2. **Be Patient with Results**:Significant change doesn't happen overnight. Trust the process and focus on the progress you're making, no matter how small it seems.

3. **Adapt When Necessary**:Life is unpredictable, and rigid plans can fail in the face of change. The long game requires flexibility—adjust your habits as your circumstances evolve.

4. **Celebrate Milestones**:While the ultimate goal might take years to achieve, acknowledging the milestones along the way keeps you motivated and engaged.

The Compounding Effect of the Long Game

One of the most powerful aspects of playing the long game is the compounding effect. Small improvements, repeated consistently, lead to exponential growth over time.

For example:

- Reading a few pages each night might not seem impactful

today, but over a decade, it could mean finishing hundreds of books.

- Spending 15 minutes a day learning a new skill might feel insignificant now, but in a year, you could be fluent in a new language or proficient in a new craft.

The compounding effect works for or against you. Just as small positive habits can create incredible results over time, small negative habits—like skipping workouts or overspending—can accumulate into significant setbacks. The long game requires intentionality in choosing the habits that define your life.

Resilience is the secret weapon of the long game. Challenges and setbacks are inevitable, but those who succeed are the ones who persist despite them.

When progress feels slow, remind yourself of your "why." Reflect on how your habits align with your long-term goals and values. This sense of purpose can sustain you through moments of doubt.

Living the Long Game

The long game isn't just a concept—it's a way of life. It's about committing to small, consistent actions that align with your values and goals, even when immediate results aren't visible.

To live the long game:

1. **Define Your Vision**: What kind of life are you building, and how do your daily actions contribute to it?

2. **Stay Consistent**: Focus on progress, not perfection, and

embrace the small wins that move you forward.

3. **Be Flexible**: Life is unpredictable. Adjust your habits and goals as needed without losing sight of the bigger picture.

The Long Game Never Ends

The beauty of the long game is that it's not about reaching a finish line—it's about continuously growing, learning, and improving. Each habit you build, each goal you achieve, becomes part of a larger journey that shapes the person you're becoming.

Are you ready to commit to the long game? Take the first step today, and trust that each small action will lead to something extraordinary over time.

Mastering Habit Synergy

Most people think of habits as individual routines, like exercising, meditating, or planning their day. But when habits are isolated, they operate like solo players on a team—they contribute, but they don't truly collaborate.

Habit synergy changes that. It's not just about building habits in isolation; it's about designing a system where your habits actively reinforce and amplify each other. While **Habit Stacking** focuses on linking habits sequentially and **The Ripple Effect** highlights the unintended benefits of a single habit, habit synergy takes it a step further: it's about creating an intentional, interconnected web of routines that work together to fuel your growth.

This approach transforms your habits from isolated achievements into a symphony of growth, creating exponential results that align with your goals, values, and aspirations.

Distinguishing Synergy from Stacking and Ripple Effects

To fully grasp synergy, let's first understand how it differs from related concepts:

1. **Habit Stacking Creates Sequences:** Habit stacking is like lining up dominoes, where each habit triggers the next. For instance, brushing your teeth leads to flossing, which leads to rinsing with mouthwash. Stacking is linear and focuses on building routines by leveraging cues from existing habits.

2. **The Ripple Effect Expands Outcomes:** The Ripple Effect refers to the unintended positive consequences of a habit. For example, a daily walk might lead to better mood and improved relationships because you're less irritable. Ripple effects are powerful but incidental—they happen as a natural byproduct, not by design.

3. **Habit Synergy Builds Systems:** Synergy, by contrast, is deliberate. It's about designing habits to complement and enhance each other, creating loops where progress in one area directly supports growth in another. Synergy transforms individual habits into a cohesive system that aligns with your life's broader goals.

In short, habit synergy is the culmination of stacking and ripple effects but taken to a new level of intentionality and integration. It's about creating a network of habits that amplify one another and work together to sustain exponential growth.

The Anatomy of Habit Synergy

Habit synergy occurs when one habit reinforces or enhances another. This connection often starts unintentionally—like realizing that better sleep improves your mood, which makes it easier to tackle work projects. But by intentionally designing habits to complement one another, you can maximize their impact.

Take Rina, a language tutor who wanted to balance her professional and personal goals. She began by habit-stacking: tying her morning tea to a 15-minute journaling session. Over time, she added another layer: using the insights from her journal to guide her daily teaching approach. By the end of each week, she reviewed her journal for patterns, identifying ways to improve her methods and manage stress. These interconnected habits didn't just improve her productivity—they aligned her personal growth with her career.

Synergistic habits aren't limited to professional success. They enhance health, relationships, and emotional resilience by creating feedback loops that reinforce positivity and momentum.

Designing a Habit Ecosystem

A habit ecosystem is a network of routines that interact seamlessly, each one supporting the others. To build your own ecosystem, you need to look beyond individual goals and consider how your habits connect to your larger values and priorities.

Start With Core Habits: Core habits are the foundational routines that drive your day. These might include exercise, sleep, or reflection. Identify one or two habits that serve as anchors for your life, then use them as the starting point for your ecosystem.

Identify Reinforcing Habits: Consider which routines naturally pair with your core habits. For instance, if exercise is a core habit, a complementary habit might be preparing meals that support your fitness goals. Reinforcing habits don't need to be complex—they just need to align with your bigger picture.

Create Feedback Loops: Feedback loops occur when the success of one habit directly boosts another. For example, spending time in nature might enhance your creativity, which leads to better journaling, which in turn deepens your mindfulness practices. The key is to recognize these connections and cultivate them intentionally.

Review and Adapt: An ecosystem isn't static—it evolves. Periodically assess how your habits are interacting. Are there gaps or redundancies? Could new routines enhance your ecosystem? By staying flexible, you ensure that your habits continue to serve your goals.

The Power of Keystone Habits

Keystone habits are unique because their influence extends beyond the routine itself. They spark ripple effects that transform other areas of life. For instance, regular exercise is often cited as a keystone habit because it doesn't just improve physical health—it boosts energy, sharpens focus, and fosters self-discipline.

Consider Andy, an architect juggling demanding projects and family responsibilities. While he loved his work, the constant deadlines and client meetings left him feeling drained and creatively stuck. He longed to reconnect with the passion that had first drawn him to architecture—the joy of sketching and imagining new designs—but finding the time felt impossible.

Determined to make a change, Andy committed to a small but powerful habit: sketching for 15 minutes each evening before bed. It wasn't about completing detailed blueprints or polished drawings—just putting pen to paper and letting his imagination wander.

At first, it felt like a small act, almost insignificant compared to the demands of his work and home life. But within a week, Andy noticed a difference. Those few minutes of sketching became his favorite part of the day—a moment of quiet creativity that felt entirely his own.

What surprised him most were the ripple effects. Sketching helped him unwind, clearing his mind after a hectic day. The habit also sparked ideas that carried over into his projects, making him feel more inspired and engaged at work. Even his family noticed the shift. His wife commented on how much calmer and more present he seemed in the evenings, and his young son often joined him, scribbling alongside on his own paper.

Over time, Andy's small habit became a cornerstone of his routine. It not only reignited his creativity but also brought unexpected benefits to his personal and professional life. That simple, daily practice of sketching reminded him of why he'd fallen in love with architecture in the first place, and it provided the energy and clarity he needed to thrive in other areas of his life.

Andy's story highlights the power of keystone habits—those small but transformative practices that create momentum and foster growth across multiple domains. By committing to one habit that fuels your passion, you can unlock a rhythm that enriches your work, your relationships, and your well-being.

Advanced Habit Stacking: Beyond the Basics

Habit stacking isn't just about linking one routine to another—it's about layering habits into clusters that align with different parts of your day. Think of it as creating "micro ecosystems" that optimize your morning, afternoon, or evening.

For example, Kayla, a small business owner, developed a morning cluster designed to set her day on the right track. It started with five minutes of deep breathing, followed by a brief journal entry outlining her priorities, and ended with reviewing her calendar. These interconnected habits created a seamless transition from waking up to diving into work, ensuring she started each day with clarity and focus.

By grouping habits based on timing or purpose, you create natural transitions that minimize decision fatigue and keep momentum high.

Synergy in the Long Term

Habit synergy isn't just about efficiency—it's about sustainability. When habits work together, they reduce the cognitive load of maintaining them. This makes it easier to stay consistent, even during challenging periods.

Think of habits as threads in a tapestry. Individually, each thread is important, but it's the connections between them that create strength and beauty. Over time, a well-designed habit ecosystem becomes a part of your identity, reinforcing who you are and what you value.

Reflection: Mapping Your Ecosystem

To harness habit synergy, start by visualizing your current routines.

Ask yourself:

- Which habits anchor my day?

- How do these habits interact with one another?

- Are there routines that could connect more effectively?

Consider using a simple diagram to map your habit ecosystem, identifying the connections and gaps. This exercise helps you see the big picture, revealing opportunities to enhance synergy and align your habits with your goals.

Your Symphony of Growth

Throughout this book, we've explored the incredible power of small habits, the science that underpins them, and the strategies that turn fleeting efforts into lasting change. Now, as you reflect on everything you've learned, it's time to see your habits not as isolated routines but as interconnected pieces of a greater whole.

Mastering habit synergy isn't just about efficiency or productivity—it's about designing a life that resonates with who you are and what you value most. It's about creating a system where every action you take builds momentum, where your habits don't just support your goals but amplify your growth in ways you never imagined.

But synergy doesn't mean perfection. There will be times when routines falter or life disrupts your carefully designed ecosystem. That's okay. Habits are tools, not rules. They're meant to adapt, evolve, and grow with you. What matters is your commitment to the process and your willingness to keep showing up, one small step at a time.

A Challenge for the Road

As you close this book, I invite you to pause and reflect. What does your ideal habit ecosystem look like? What values, goals, and dreams do you want it to nurture? Start small. Choose one core habit to anchor your system, then gradually layer in routines that reinforce and expand it.

Remember, habits aren't just about what you do—they're about who you become. With each action, you're casting a vote for the person you aspire to be. And with every connection you create between your habits, you're designing a life that reflects your values, your vision, and your potential.

The Journey Ahead

You now have the tools to transform your life, one micro habit at a time. But this is just the beginning. Habits are a lifelong journey—a process of continuous refinement, discovery, and growth. As you move forward, trust in the power of small steps. Trust in the ripple effects that come from a single action. And trust in the synergy that happens when your habits align with your highest self.

Your symphony of growth awaits. It's time to take the first step.

www.ingramcontent.com/pod-product-compliance
Lightning Source LLC
Chambersburg PA
CBHW071541220526
45469CB00003B/874